MINDFUL
BEAUTY

About the Authors

Debbie Palmer, DO, is a New York-based, board-certified dermatologist with more than nineteen years of experience. She is the medical director and cofounder of Dermatology Associates of New York and the founder of Replere skincare. Dr. Palmer is one of only several hundred dermatologists in the country also trained in osteopathic medicine—a holistic philosophy and approach that relates each part of the body to the entire system.

Dr. Palmer graduated with a BBA from the University of Michigan and earned her medical degree *summa cum laude* from Kansas City University. She completed her residency in dermatology at St. Barnabas Hospital in Bronx, New York.

Dr. Palmer is author of two books in addition to *Mindful Beauty*: *Beyond Beauty* and *The Dermatologists' Prescription for a New You!* She is the recipient of various book awards including the NYC Big Book Award, the Pinnacle Book Achievement Award, the Independent Press Award, and the Coalition of Visionary Resources Gold and Silver Winner. Dr. Palmer has also been featured in numerous national publications and radio shows and on television.

Valerie Latona is the former editor in chief of *Shape* and served as an advisor to the Office of Research on Women's Health at the National Institutes of Health. Her work as a health and wellness writer and editor has been featured in publications such as *Prevention*, *Women's Health*, and *Yoga Journal*.

MiNDFUL BEAUTY

Holistic Habits to Feel and Look Your Best

DR. DEBBIE PALMER
WITH VALERIE LATONA

LLEWELLYN PUBLICATIONS
WOODBURY, MINNESOTA

First Edition
First Printing, 2020

Book design: Samantha Penn
Cover design: Shira Atakpu
Editing: Annie Burdick

Llewellyn Publications is a registered trademark of Llewellyn Worldwide Ltd.

Library of Congress Cataloging-in-Publication Data (Pending)
ISBN: 978-0-7387-61862

Llewellyn Publications
A Division of Llewellyn Worldwide Ltd.
2143 Wooddale Drive
Woodbury, MN 55125-2989
www.llewellyn.com

Printed in the United States of America

Other Books by Debbie Palmer

Beyond Beauty

The Dermatologists' Prescription for a New You!

To my husband and best friend Sergio. Boundless gratitude for your unconditional love and support and for your adventurous spirit that helps nourish my soul's journey. I couldn't have done this without you.

And to my children Matthew and Michael who have taught me so much and given me the greatest love.

CONTENTS

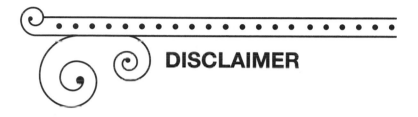

DISCLAIMER

READERS ARE URGED TO consult their health care provider or medical practitioner before undertaking any new diet, fitness program, or lifestyle change. The information in this book is for educational purposes only. It is not intended to replace the advice of your physician or medical practitioner. Although every effort has been made to provide the best possible information in this book, the authors are not responsible for accidents, injury, or damage incurred as a result of attempting any of the activities or steps recommended here.

ACKNOWLEDGMENTS

I WOULD LIKE TO thank my husband and children for making our house a home filled with love and happiness. You show me the meaning of love every single day.

I thank my team at work for giving it your all and for making our office feel like family. Jennifer, Lauren, Deb, Maria, Jackie, Marjorie, and Taylor: you are all amazing and I appreciate everything you do. Thank you, Dan, for all your creativity and for always being there.

To all my patients: you've given me the greatest privilege of getting to know both you and your families. Thank you for including me in your lives and allowing me to help guide you on your journey to wellness.

A very special thank you to everyone at Llewellyn. Thank you, Bill, for believing in me and helping my dream come to life. Thank you, Amy, Terry, Leah, Kat, Anna, Annie, and Sami. You have all been a delight to work with and I am beyond grateful for your support.

To all my teachers, professors, and attending physicians: sharing your knowledge and experience with me has been invaluable. Thank you for being my role models. It was you who assisted me in accomplishing my goal of becoming a physician, something that I had dreamed of since I was in the sixth grade. Cindy, it was you who opened my world to dermatology.

Thank you, too, to all my friends in Michigan, Florida, Missouri, New York, and Connecticut. I'm blessed to have you in my life. I'm doubly blessed for my extended family in Michigan. I love you all!

And lastly, thank you to my coauthor Valerie Latona for helping me bring to life the topics that I talk about daily with patients. Thank you for your friendship, dedication, and endless hours of help. We are two wellness-minded peas in a pod.

INTRODUCTION

DESPITE ALL THE MODERN conveniences of today—faster computers, smartphones, groceries delivered to our doorstep, and cooking gadgets that shave off time—our lives are busier than ever. What's more, work and family needs, financial demands, daily life to-dos, emails, and social media pressures are leaving less introspective "me time" and relaxation time than ever before. This daily stress, without the necessary restorative work to offset it, is draining to our spirit, mind, and body, and our outer radiance. I see this daily in my practice as a dermatologist in New York. Patients come to me stressed and looking for a quick-fix solution—whether a topical cream, an injectable to erase wrinkles, a laser treatment, or something else—to look younger and healthier and to feel more confident about themselves. While I do offer all of these options, there's a key component of beauty, which I refer to as *mindful beauty*, that's so often missing today: a mind, body, and soul-nourishing lifestyle that's essential for inner peace and outer beauty. Because of the 24/7 demands on us due to our modern lifestyles, it's easy to be less present in the moment and therefore less aware of what our bodies and our spirits truly need to thrive. But what we're putting into our bodies and doing to our body on a daily basis, as well as the health of our spiritual life, are all as critical to beauty and aging gracefully as what we're doing to the outside of our bodies. In fact, they're even more important. That's where this book comes in.

All of the information that I have culled from years of working with patients is included in the pages of this book, along with some of the latest studies linking spirituality, nutrition, and health to stress reduction and glowing skin.

I'm confident about what works to help people look and feel better because I've seen the results in so many patients of different ages, lifestyles, and cultures whom I've had the privilege of treating. Over the past nineteen years that I've been practicing dermatology, I've helped thousands of patients have healthier, more peaceful, and more spiritually aware lives. As one of just several hundred dermatologists in the country also trained in osteopathic medicine, I am uniquely qualified to connect the systems within the body and to understand how stress triggers an imbalance in the body that is also reflected on the skin. Osteopathy is a holistic, preventive approach to medicine that believes each part of the body, including the skin, is linked to every other part. Osteopaths like myself have a four-year medical degree just like any medical doctor, along with three to seven years of residency, but we also have additional training in osteopathy. It's this insight that has given me the ability to explain how what we do to our bodies and spirits affects our overall beauty, both inside and out.

Inner and Outer Beauty

Take Kate, for example. Kate is a patient of mine who was stressed in her job. She had put on weight over the previous couple of years, due to on-the-go eating, a lack of regular restorative sleep, and no time for regular, consistent exercise, not to mention practically non-existent "me" time. Not only did Kate look tired and worn out, but she also looked years older than she actually was. She came to me to help her look younger. We talked about a lot of things, including the important elements of beauty, health, and anti-aging that Kate wasn't paying attention to in her daily life: stress reduction, spirituality, healthy relationships, diet, and sleep. Kate was like so many of us who live lifestyles dictated by stressful jobs that leave little time for the key components of healthy living, specifically:

- Taking time out to relax mentally *and* physically
- Spiritual enrichment
- Eating a diet rich in nourishing, whole, unprocessed foods
- Moving the body every day
- Getting enough restful sleep
- Learning to develop a passion for life again
- Nurturing healthy relationships

After sitting and talking with Kate, we worked out a skincare plan for her, but we also established a realistic lifestyle plan, one that worked with the demands of her work and her life. One of the key components of this lifestyle makeover was that Kate had to take at least thirty consecutive minutes for herself every day to spend how she liked, away from her phone, her emails, her family, even the pile of laundry waiting to be folded. It was up to her whether she took this time to meditate, exercise, do some simple yoga stretches, sit quietly with a cup of tea, or take a reflective walk outdoors. But these thirty minutes were non-negotiable and critical to reducing the stress in her life. Think about it: most of us are awake more than fifteen hours a day. Spending thirty minutes on yourself is actually not much at all. But it's an important step to making yourself a priority, which is a key factor in helping to bring balance back into your life. While we were sitting there in my office together, Kate added "me time" to her schedule on her phone as a recurring daily event. What Kate found, which she explained to me later, was that making this time for herself was a simple change, she began to look forward to it, and it made a big difference for her overall anxiety levels. She began to sleep better and, because she wasn't always exhausted, she also started making healthier food choices.

One of my core beliefs is that when you begin to reduce the stress in your life, everything changes: your confidence increases, your outlook on life becomes more positive, you have more energy, you sleep better, your relationships improve, and yes, the appearance and health of your skin improves too. When Kate came back to me several months later, she looked more radiant and she was much happier. Things hadn't miraculously changed overnight, but her whole attitude had become more positive over time. She even told me that her thirty minutes of "me time" had now become an hour every day: thirty minutes in the morning and thirty minutes at night. This is consistently what I see with all my patients who undertake a stress-reducing lifestyle makeover. What you do to rebalance yourself—therefore reducing tension in your life—will absolutely improve how you look on the outside. This is true inner and outer mindful beauty.

Exactly How This Book Will Help You

In this book, I'm going to walk you through proven ways to incorporate healthier habits and how to slowly and gradually balance out your life so you're healthier and more spiritually connected. Your skin will look years younger too. Like Kate, you'll also have a more positive outlook on life, because there's a genuine happiness and self-confidence that comes when you're less tense and anxious and all parts of your body are working together in harmony.

First, though, I'd like you to step back and take a moment to reflect on who you are. Close your eyes and take several deep breaths in and out. As you breathe in deeply, appreciate all that you have and are. As you breathe out, let go of any worries, fears, and insecurities about your life, your health, your body. Acceptance of who you are and all your amazing qualities is critical for self-acceptance, but also to motivate you to put into practice, and stick to, the healthy changes suggested in this book. For you, this moment of appreciation can be something that you do in the morning and/or before bed. It will leave you feeling good about who you are and less bothered with day-to-day concerns.

Now take a moment to think about the things you'd like to do to be a healthier, happier you. Be sure to reflect on how you feel spiritually and emotionally, something that most people forget to take into account because it's less tangible. Do you wake up every morning with energy and joy? Do you feel fulfilled with your social connections and relationships? Do you take time to slow down and connect with your inner or higher self? Are you mindful several times throughout the day with all of your awareness in the here and now?

Now turn your attention to your sleep habits and energy levels. How much shut-eye are you getting every night, and do you wake up feeling rested and recharged? Do you feel lively or sluggish? Be sure to ponder, too, your diet and your exercise habits. All these things either encourage stress or feed the mind, body, and spirit. Be honest with yourself about the things you're doing that are benefitting you and those that are not. Think about everything and, if you need to, write these things down. These words will be important motivation to keep you on track throughout this process of inner growth and outer transformation. Sometimes it requires a heartfelt inner conversation to get the answers to questions like these. Take all the time you need. Responding to these questions honestly will help you move forward with acceptance.

Whatever you do, though, don't judge yourself. Every one of us has habits that could be "better." You are unique, wonderful, and one of a kind. Don't forget this. Just answer these questions honestly and without self-criticism. If you start to judge yourself, just bring your thoughts back to the fact that you are unique and wonderful and that this process is a journey to rebalance your life and awaken all the potential you have inside.

Throughout the course of this book, I'll work with you at replacing stress-inducing unhealthy habits with healthier ones that leave you feeling more centered. It isn't easy to stop ingrained habits, but taking small steps to change—what Kate tried with her thirty minutes a day and what this book offers—is what will result in success. Throughout this book, you'll find easy tips to incorporate into your life. You do not need to put all of them into practice at once. The idea is that you can create a lifestyle makeover that works for you and your life. And this might mean just one change or it might be three or more. All I ask is that you commit to yourself and don't give up.

One of my favorite mantras is "Old, negative patterns of eating, living, and working will no longer limit me."

Make this saying your motivational mantra as you journey on this path toward inner and outer mindful beauty.

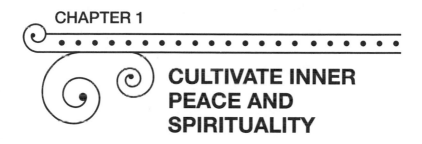

CHAPTER 1

CULTIVATE INNER PEACE AND SPIRITUALITY

STRESS. WE ALL EXPERIENCE IT. No matter how "perfect" someone's life or social media posts may seem, no one is immune to stress. It's a normal, almost expected, part of daily life today thanks to busy family lives, work pressures, being connected to our phones and computers 24/7, financial ups and downs, relationship issues, and health issues. Pretty much everything in our busy lives can trigger stress, both emotional and physical. Even good experiences like running a race, giving a speech, or celebrating a big event can cause stress.

What's common in all these situations is that they require a response from us. In fact, it's how we respond to stressful situations that determines how stress affects us. If we get angry, frustrated, or sad and depressed; think about things over and over and lose sleep; and/or let what's happening in our lives affect our relationships, then the stress will only persist, triggering more of a reaction in our bodies, referred to as the body's stress response. But if we allow stressful situations to exist and simply pass without much reaction from us, the stress is short-lived. This is my goal for you with this book: I want to help you, as I do with all my patients, to look at and react to stress differently, using the tools I describe on the pages ahead.

Your body's stress response is a natural one: it's your internal alarm system (the so-called "flight or fight" response) that prepares you to fight a perceived stressor or run from it. But you can control how long it lasts. Your stress response can be short-lived, which doesn't take as great a physical toll on you because your body has a chance to recover from it. Stress responses can also be chronic, in which case there is very little recuperation time and plenty of wear and tear on your body and mind over time. This is what occurs with so many of us today, but it doesn't need to be the case. With the right tools in your daily-life arsenal, you can react to stress differently. A more even-keeled response will result in a healthier, happier you—and more beautifully radiant skin.

How Stress Affects the Body and the Skin

When we experience long-term chronic stress, the health of our body and our skin can suffer. Our spirit can get worn down too, depleting our inner strength and outer radiance as well as our hope and happiness. But recognizing how stress affects the body and the spirit will help you understand how and why it can (but doesn't need to) trigger health problems and affect longevity. Consider how stress is affecting us, from the American Psychological Association:

- 43 percent of all adults suffer adverse health effects from stress
- 75 percent to 90 percent of all doctor's office visits are for stress-related ailments and complaints
- 40 percent of adults lay awake at night because of stress

When the body encounters a perceived stressor, be it a looming deadline or a fight with a spouse, the body responds accordingly. The hypothalamus (the part of the brain responsible for hormone production) communicates with the adrenal glands situated above the kidneys, alerting them to pump out stress hormones like cortisol and epinephrine or adrenaline. These hormones help get the body ready to react.

When these hormones are released, the liver produces more glucose or blood sugar to provide the body with extra energy. Our muscles tense up, the body's way of guarding against injury and pain (why hands-on relaxation techniques like massage can help). We also start to breathe rapidly. We're entering full-on panic mode. If you're starting to feel stressed just reading these symptoms, stop reading and take three long, slow breaths in and out. Breathe in while quietly counting to four, hold your breath for a count of seven, and then breathe out while quietly counting to eight. You feel better, right? It's amazing what stopping to consciously breathe can do. This is one of the most effective tools in your stress-busting arsenal because it puts the brakes on your body's stress response. Taking deep breaths in and out (which I discuss more throughout this book) is also a way to put yourself back in control of a stressful situation. It costs nothing and requires nothing except for you to stop and breathe. And you can do it anywhere: in your car during a traffic jam, at work before a big meeting, or at home when interacting with family members. Keep this in mind as you encounter stress in your life.

These same stress hormones that cause you to breathe rapidly also cause an increase in heart rate and stronger contractions of the heart muscle. The blood vessels that direct blood to the large muscles and the heart dilate, increasing the amount of blood being pumped though the body. The result can get more blood to your heart and muscles to help you to run faster if you're in a race (a good thing!), but when chronic it can trigger increased blood pressure.

Under stress, your body also releases a protein called neuropeptide S or NPS, which decreases sleep and increases alertness. The body is essentially keeping you awake and alert to face the danger it senses. So, if you wonder why you're tossing and turning or waking up in the middle of the night and having trouble going back to sleep, stress is a likely culprit. At night before bed, or even in the middle of the night when you wake up, go back to the deep breathing technique I just mentioned. This can be a helpful sleep aid. By taking time to breathe deeply, you not only interrupt the body's stress but you also allow your body to relax, which inevitably lets you drift back off to sleep.

All these reactions in the body can trigger both emotional and physical problems, particularly when they're being activated for long periods of time. Long-term stress has been linked to everything from depression, anxiety, and headaches to heart attacks, strokes, and type 2 diabetes. It's also been associated with gastrointestinal disturbances like constipation, ulcers, irritable bowel syndrome (IBS), and colitis. (APA, 2018)

Scientists from around the world believe that too much chronic stress can reduce our lifespan by causing age-related deterioration in our bodies. In a nutshell, stress causes us to age faster. Researchers at Oregon State University are studying this relationship between stress and aging. One connection they found has to do with something called telomeres. Telomeres are cap-like structures at the end of a chromosome or genetic material in each of our cells. They protect the end of the chromosome from deteriorating. The researchers found that those under extreme stress have shorter telomeres than others. When telomeres get too short, the cell can no longer divide and tissue can't regenerate any more. (OregonLive, 2012) This shortening process or "internal clock" is associated with aging, say researchers at Stanford University Medical Center. (Broughton et al, 2005)

The younger you are, the longer these telomeres should be. Lifestyle factors, such as smoking and consumption of sugary processed food and drinks, have all been linked to having shorter telomeres. It stands to reason then that eating fewer processed and sugary foods and more whole foods like fruits, vegetables, whole grains, healthy fats, and lean proteins can help keep your telomeres longer. This is a growing area of research today, and I believe we've just started to see how important these telomeres are to every single aspect of our health. (University of Utah, 2019)

Reducing stress and living a healthy, fulfilled life can help keep telomeres longer too. In fascinating research from Howard University Medical Center, for example, it was found that regular practice of transcendental meditation or mantra meditation stimulates genes to produce telomerase, an enzyme that adds molecules to the ends of telomeres to lengthen them and protect them from deteriorating. (Eureka Alert, 2015) So not only can meditation relax you and focus your mind, it can also truly keep you young! (Read more on these meditations in chapter two.) Each of us can find techniques like meditation and breathing that work to help us get a handle on stress. We can find ways to control our stress response with techniques that are easy to learn and easy to put into practice so that stress doesn't trigger long-term problems. I share what's worked for me and for my patients throughout this book. (Duraimani et al, 2005)

Stress and the Skin

My patient Michael, an attorney, was under a lot of pressure at work. He noticed that every time he had a big trial coming up, his psoriasis would get considerably worse, with red and white, patchy, scaling skin all over his body. It bothered him, as did the incredibly long hours he was putting in at work, but he didn't think he had the time to address it. It was Michael's wife who encouraged him to see a dermatologist. That's when Michael booked an appointment with me.

When Michael came into my office, his psoriasis was in full flare-up mode. We spoke about his condition and how we could treat it with prescription medication, but we also spoke about the importance of taking better care of himself: healthy eating, stress-reduction techniques, regular exercise, and just simply taking time for himself, which is something so many of us forget about in today's hectic life. Psoriasis may be a chronic disease, but combining a healthy lifestyle with treatment can absolutely reduce the symptoms and flare-ups. I see this all the time with patients in my office. By changing how they live their lives, they can also improve the health of their skin and their bodies.

During stressful times, neurotransmitters or brain chemicals that communicate information throughout your brain and body are released, triggering stress-related responses like inflammation of the skin, which is the largest organ in the body. The result can be a worsening of skin problems like acne, eczema, and psoriasis if you aren't taking steps to mitigate the stress. Stress-triggered inflammation can also contribute to premature aging of the skin, including fine lines and wrinkles. If the stress is chronic— and again, with the right coping tools in place, it doesn't have to be—the skin's barrier function is also compromised, allowing irritants to enter through the skin, and allowing moisture to escape. This is why stressed skin gets dry, rough, and dull. Researchers at Mt. Sinai School of Medicine in New York believe this impaired skin barrier function is also linked to slower wound healing and increased susceptibility to infections. This is why, when a patient comes to me to discuss their skin problems, I ask them about their lifestyle. I know that if together we can come up with techniques that will help them de-stress, their skin problems have more of a chance of clearing up for good. (Lebwohl et al, 2005)

How We React to Stress

Michael took my words to heart and made a conscious decision to start taking care of himself. When he came back for his follow-up several months later, he looked like a different person. His skin was clear and had been for several weeks, and he felt better than ever. Michael had started exercising thirty minutes in the morning several days a week at his company gym, which he had never taken advantage of before. Instead of catching up on TV shows on his computer during lunch, he started meditating. Michael started eating better too, reaching more for fruits and vegetables rather than processed grab-and-go snacks. He wasn't perfect, and no one is. There were days when he didn't fit in a workout or meditation and there were plenty of days when he reached for his favorite chips as a mid-afternoon snack, but overall his entire lifestyle and approach to life improved. He explained to me that not only did his skin improve, but so did his clarity of mind. He found that, as a result of the changes he made, he was more focused and productive at work. He was also happier overall, which affected his relationships at work and at home.

Like Michael, when we're under stress and functioning in crisis mode, we tend to slack on healthy habits such as getting enough sleep, exercising, and sticking to a healthy diet. This is understandable. We're all human. It's hard to reach for an apple when a warm chocolate chip cookie holds more comforting appeal. This is okay to grab once in a while, but persistent unhealthy choices over time can further fuel stress. Unhealthy foods that contain empty calories and lack key nutrients can trigger low mental and physical energy, which makes it hard to get things done. Not getting things done can trigger more stress. Processed foods in general, which include so many of the foods we reach for during stressful times, can trigger addictive eating, which makes you want to eat more. Not moving your body can also make you less motivated and less confident. If the stress and lack of activity is short lived, the effects on the body aren't severe. But when stress and lack of activity are chronic, these unhealthy habits can make us more predisposed to despair, weight gain, and premature aging.

It's important to be able to recognize the causes of stress in our lives and to manage them. Some stressors cannot be eliminated entirely, though, and this is when our frame of mind becomes critical. We can control how we react to a situation that's beyond our control. Don't let a difficult person or situation steal your peace. How we perceive a situation, as well as how we react to it, makes a difference in whether we're relaxed or we trigger our stress response. We've all seen an example of this when stuck in a traffic jam. Some people react with anger and aggression, honking their horn and yelling out the window about the prospect of being late for wherever they're headed, and others are able to sit back, listen to the radio, and accept the possibility of being delayed. With practice, we can shape our natural tendencies and react to things differently. One way to do this is by repeating a mantra like this (or one of your choosing) when you're under stress: "I will not let this situation affect my peace." (Ovetakin-White et al, 2019)

Stress and Vitamin C

Whatever you do, be sure to get enough vitamin C on a daily basis. You can find this key nutrient in fruits like oranges, papayas, and strawberries, and in vegetables like red and green peppers, broccoli, Brussels sprouts, and asparagus. Here's why you need it: Stress, particularly if it's intense and prolonged, rapidly depletes vitamin C from the body. In fact, one of the highest concentrations of vitamin C in the body is found in the adrenal glands, which play a central role in dealing with stress. It's not surprising then that vitamin C helps reduce both the psychological and physical effects of stress. This vitamin seems to counteract or even prevent secretion of the key stress hormone cortisol that's responsible for triggering the "flight or fight" response to stress. Vitamin C is also responsible for protecting blood vessels, helping to create the skin-firming protein collagen, and supporting the immune system. (Blaylock, 2015)

Stress and Weight Gain: The Truth

It turns out there's a lot of truth behind the whole idea of stress eating, and it may have little to do with our willpower or lack of it. In the short term, stress can shut down appetite. When under stress, the hypothalamus produces a hormone that suppresses hunger. Adrenaline, produced by the adrenal glands, also temporarily puts eating on hold. But if stress persists, then this normal stress response goes haywire. Elevated levels of the stress hormone cortisol begin to trigger our sugar and carbohydrate cravings. This is why chronic stress can actually increase the appetite, thanks to cortisol. And it's not healthy fruits and veggies that we crave. It's sugar and fat like cookies, candy, cake, chips, and fries. In fact, this desire for comfort foods may be a biological way of feeding the body enough energy to sustain the stress response long term. These highly processed foods can, in turn, also fuel addictive eating. What ensues is a vicious cycle of binging and addictive eating that can challenge even those of us with the toughest willpower. Eating this way over the long haul can pack on pounds, particularly in the abdominal area, which can lead to cardiovascular disease, type 2 diabetes, and stroke. But it doesn't have to. As I mentioned, by controlling our response to stress, we can stop this whole binge eating reaction in its tracks. Think about it: if, instead of reaching for a cookie when a work deadline is looming, you took a deep breath and walked outside for five minutes, you would turn the tables on the stress response and regain control of the situation. Your reaction is controlled by you.

Complementary and alternative healing therapies, which I talk about later in this chapter, are an effective way to get stress and anxiety under control. With this in mind, everyone needs to find ways to reduce stress and find new ways to eat for energy during times of stress. (Schulte et al, 2015)

Eat to Beat Stress

A well-balanced diet can help you function your best during times of stress. Some ways to avoid unhealthy stress-induced eating that have worked for me and my patients are included here.

Prepare your pantry and fridge. If you tend to reach for the fastest meal while under stress, then stock your kitchen with quick, healthy food options. This can include fruits, vegetables, hard-boiled eggs, yogurt (dairy or non-dairy), nuts and seeds, healthy grains like rice cakes and air-popped popcorn, and healthy, protein-rich dips like hummus. You can also cook extra portions of healthy meals on the weekends that can be quickly re-heated during the week. Try to avoid buying foods you know are unhealthy so they won't be an option during stressful times.

Keep healthy restaurants on speed dial. Knowing ahead of time where the healthy restaurant options are in your area can help you avoid unhealthy eating pit stops. Also, take a look at the menus at these restaurants so you have nutrient-packed standbys when you're in a rush. Sarah, one of my patients who was struggling with persistent acne, explained how this tip helped her change her diet for the better. A sales rep responsible for driving around to different clients all day, Sarah started becoming proactive about where she could pick up healthier meals. Once she started doing this, she lost some of the extra pounds she had put on since she started her job, her skin cleared up, and she had more energy and enthusiasm for life. It's truly amazing how a change in diet can result in such a pronounced change in the body, the skin, and the spirit!

Swap out unhealthy snacks. We're all familiar with the sugar and processed food cravings that accompany stress, but stopping these anxiety-provoked binges before they start will keep your energy and mood up and keep your skin radiant and more youthful looking. Instead, try mixing protein with a fruit or grain (for example, an apple with a nut or seed butter, homemade trail mix with nuts, seeds, and dried fruits, or string cheese and crackers). It's the protein that will keep you satisfied and the fruit and grains that will help satiate your cravings.

Take a moment to relax. So much of unhealthy eating starts with mindless eating: munching while working on a project, eating while talking on the phone or watching TV, snacking when anxious and distracted. If you take a moment to step back from your mindless craving and break away from the situation, you'll find that your need to eat is lessened, as is your stress. Taking a walk around your office or outside or just closing your eyes to breathe deeply are proven ways to shift the focus of your mind and help you relax. (Mandal, 2019)

Breathing for Stress Relief

Breathing is the only function of the body that we perform both voluntarily and involuntarily. As I mentioned earlier, controlling the breath is a powerful technique, also called pranayama, that's a major component of yoga and meditation and is critical to good health. (*Prana* is the Sanskrit word for breath, spirit, or universal energy.) Through it, we can regulate anxiety, improve sleep and energy levels, and reduce stress. It can also regulate heart rate, blood pressure, circulation, and digestion. Not only can it help physical and emotional health, but it is an integral part of mindfulness and spiritual awareness.

Diaphragmatic breathing, in particular, helps calm the body and the mind. The diaphragm, called the most efficient muscle of breathing, is the large dome-shaped muscle located at the base of the lungs. Diaphragmatic breathing (deep, slow breathing that originates from below this muscle and travels upward into the chest area), as opposed to shallow breathing from the chest (how most of us breathe and a hallmark of anxiety), has been used for thousands of years as a way to enhance health and even spiritual practices.

Diaphragmatic breathing is how we breathe from the time we're born, but then our breaths become shallower as we get older and start to experience more stress. Also called yoga breathing, diaphragmatic breathing is both a form of meditation and a preparation for deep meditation. To perform diaphragmatic breathing, try the following steps:

Find a quiet place, get comfortable, and start by relaxing your head, neck, and shoulders. You can lie on your back on a flat surface, or in bed with your knees bent and your head supported. Place a pillow under your knees to support your legs, if necessary. You can also do this sitting in a chair at home or at work with your knees bent and your feet flat on the floor, head and neck relaxed.

Gently move the tip of your tongue against the roof of your mouth, just behind your upper front teeth, and inhale deeply to a mental count of four. Try to inhale from your stomach area (your diaphragm), not your chest.

Hold your breath for a count of seven. Then exhale quietly and completely through your mouth with slightly pursed lips to a count of eight. This is one breath cycle. Repeat this cycle for five minutes.

You should try to practice this breathing for five to ten minutes, one to three times per day. Some apps like *Stop, Breathe and Think*; *Paced Breathing*; and *Calm* can help you do this by sending you reminders to pause during your day to take relaxation breaths.

Take a Deep Breath and Commit to Quit Smoking

Taking long, deep breaths in and out is a common relaxation practice. It's also common practice for smokers, and taking a break from the craziness of life to do this outdoors is how smokers begin to associate smoking with relaxation. This is why so many smokers reach for a cigarette when they're stressed and why, once this habit gets ingrained and nicotine dependence sets in, it's so hard to break.

Smoking is not an easy habit to break but it *is* 100 percent possible. And you *can* do it. Just as controlling addictive stress eating can be done—by taking baby steps to change—so too can getting a handle on smoking be accomplished.

While the relaxation effect of smoking is good in theory, all those chemicals being inhaled into the body (more than seven thousand altogether) are not healthy. According to the National Cancer Institute, hundreds of these chemicals are toxic and about seventy are known to cause cancer. These include formaldehyde, benzene (found in gasoline), polonium 210 (radioactive), and vinyl chloride (used to make pipes). Plus, every one of these chemicals contributes to premature aging of the body and the skin. (Kennedy et al, 2003)

Secondhand smoke is also toxic. This smoke, according to the Centers for Disease Control and Prevention, contains the same seven thousand chemicals that smokers expose themselves to when smoking. Secondhand cigarette smoke can cause frequent and severe asthma attacks, respiratory infections, ear infections, and sudden infant death syndrome, as well as heart disease, strokes, and lung cancer. Researchers at the University of California San Francisco found that nonsmokers who sit in a car with a smoker for just one hour (even with the windows slightly open) had significantly increased levels of carcinogens and other toxins associated with cancer, heart disease, and lung disease in their urine, which means that these chemicals have entered the body. Even "thirdhand" smoke, the smoke pollutants that remain in an indoor environment on surfaces or in dust where smokers have smoked (such as a home or a car), has been shown to be dangerous to health. (Ferrante et al, 2013)

For all these reasons, it's important to commit to quit. I know it's not easy, but like any other good habit that you're trying to incorporate into your life, it takes awareness, motivation to change, and persistence. What this means is that if you slide back into old habits, you simply accept what happened without judgment and try again without giving up. Repeat as often as necessary and the good habits will eventually win out. I have seen this with so many of my patients. This is where relaxation techniques like yoga, meditation, and walking outdoors in nature can help you cope with the stresses of daily life so you have less of an urge to reach for that cigarette when life gets tough. Remember, you *are* worth the change you're going to make.

Where Do You Go from Here?

Reducing stress in your life is one of the single most important things you can do to boost your health and your overall well-being. As I've discussed, stress takes its toll on every aspect of our lives and our health—of body, mind, spirit, and skin. So many of my patients worry that taking steps to de-stress will add another to-do item to their already long to-do list. Nothing could be further from the truth. Simple, easy de-stressing tools, such as the breathing exercise I had you do, are what I want you to leave this chapter and this book with. Add in what you can when you can. What you'll find is this: once these relaxation strategies become habit, you'll find yourself looking forward to doing them and wonder how you ever survived without them.

CHAPTER 2

THINK HAPPY, BE HAPPY

BY FOLLOWING OUR HEARTS, having gratitude for all that we have, and taking time to truly enjoy every moment of every day, we can reduce stress and make a huge impact on our happiness and on our health. One of my favorite sayings, which has often been attributed to Voltaire, is "I have chosen to be happy because it is good for my health." How true this is. Just feeling positive and looking at life from a glass-half-full perspective can do wonders for your stress levels and your happiness. A big part of this is making the choice to be happy and not let the bad things in life get you down. Viktor Frankl, in *Man's Search for Meaning*, touches upon how a positive attitude allows a person to endure suffering and disappointments and can enhance satisfaction. A negative attitude, however, can worsen pain or disappointment and undermine satisfaction.

We all have the freedom to choose how we'll respond to a situation and how we approach each situation in our lives (with either a positive or a negative attitude) and this helps to shape the meaning of our lives. Research backs this up. One study, published in a journal of the American Psychological Association, found that people who are cheerful and positive in the face of stress have lower levels of inflammation in the body. Failing to maintain a positive, happy outlook had the opposite effect: elevated levels of disease-triggering inflammation, particularly in women. What's more, scientists at the University of Wisconsin–Madison found that being happy increases our antibodies—critical proteins utilized by the immune system to fight off viruses, bacteria, and more—by an incredible 50 percent. (Sin et al, 2015; Collingwood, 2014)

I would also say that people who are happier are more beautiful. They have a natural glow about them, as well as an indescribable energy that radiates from the inside out.

The Habits of Happy People

Being cheerful is contagious, for you and for everyone else around you. It's hard not to smile when someone else smiles at you. It also brings a natural radiance and beauty to your face that can't be mimicked by any skin creams or treatments. Happy people are beautiful people. They have what I call truly natural beauty.

There are four cardinal virtues, as outlined by Lao Tzu in the classic Chinese text *Tao Te Ching* that closely mimic the habits of happy people: reverence for all life, natural sincerity, gentleness, and supportiveness. According to Lao Tzu, it is through these principles that we align spiritually, and in turn receive universal guidance and support. In this way, we are able to cultivate true inner peace. I would also say it is through these principles that we can cultivate true happiness. (Power of Positivity, 2019) There is also a quote I love from Mahatma Gandhi that also speaks to this alignment as it relates to happiness: "Happiness is when what you think, what you say, and what you do are in harmony." How true this is. It's not always easy to achieve this harmony, but this is where this book comes in. Consider it your personal stress-busting, happiness-boosting beauty book.

If you're feeling less than cheerful lately, try practicing these cardinal virtues by following one or all of these habits of happy people.

1. Take time to nourish the relationships that matter.

One way to take positive steps toward happiness is through friends and family. Healthy relationships are good for us emotionally and physically. People with happy relationships have an overall positive view of life and are generally less stressed. They also have a stronger immune system, decreased health issues like heart disease, and increased longevity. In fact, researchers at Carnegie Mellon University found that just the act of hugging someone can boost your health. (Cohen et al, 2014) Sex can help reduce stress too, and even make you look younger. This is the result of the secretion, during sex, of the human growth hormone or HGH. It's this hormone that plays a key role in boosting skin elasticity. (Carter, 2013)

Pets help make people happy too, because they provide meaningful social support. There's incredible evidence, firsthand and in clinical research, that there's an emotional bond between people and animals that can have benefits on our emotional and physical health. In fact, psychologists have found that pet owners have higher self-esteem, feel less lonely, are less fearful, and are more socially outgoing, all factors that can make one less stressed and more happy. (McConnell et al, 2011) These same pet owners had a greater sense of belonging, meaningful existence, and control over their lives. I have found this in my own life. My family's two dogs bring us such joy, love, and laughter. They also remind us to be mindful and live in the moment. (McConnell, 2011)

2. Allow yourself small moments of happiness.

All it takes sometimes is a smile. Sometimes forcing yourself to smile when you least want to will change your outlook for the better. I've found that smiling makes me feel happy on the inside. A smile lights up your face and makes others happy to be around you. There's also a natural beauty in those who smile a lot.

3. Limit your daily news intake, particularly before bed.

There are so many stress-provoking stories in the news today it's no wonder people are so full of stress. While it's important to stay informed, too much news can trigger more anxiety, and the constant influx of news via social media is only adding to this stress. Try avoiding media for a few days each month and always at least an hour before going to bed each night, and see how you feel. You may find yourself less stressed and sleeping more soundly.

When it comes to what's going on in the world or even in just our own lives, I've found that these words from the theologian-philosopher Reinhold Niebuhr (repeated often or pasted up on a note by your desk or on your fridge) can often help: "God, grant me the serenity to accept the things I cannot change, the courage to change the things I can, and the wisdom to know the difference." (Chronicle of Higher Education, 2014)

4. Schedule relaxation time, even if you have to write it on your calendar.

The happiest people are those who take regular breaks from daily stress. Whether that means regular meditation, yoga, exercise, daily walks, or even just taking time for yourself to do something you enjoy, taking a break from the grind *will* make you feel more in control of your life and will contribute to you having a more positive outlook overall.

5. Carve out time to move every day.

Just as you have to schedule relaxation time, scheduling regular exercise can help make you feel happier. (And it may be that your exercise time *is* your relaxation time, so you get double the benefits.) Working out consistently has been shown in numerous studies to mimic the effects of antidepressants on the brain. When you exercise, the body releases endorphins, chemicals secreted by the hypothalamus that make you feel good. When these endorphins are released, they block the transmission of pain signals and also produce a euphoric feeling. (Scheve, 2019) Exercise has also been shown to improve sleep, enough of which can make anyone's outlook on the world rosier. (Youngstedt, 2005)

6. Be grateful for the things in your life that are going well, even if they're small and insignificant in your mind.

Waking up in the morning, a beautiful sunset, a happy tail wag and greeting from a pet, your morning cup of hot coffee, getting to work without a traffic jam. Big victories and events shouldn't be the focus in life. It's the small victories and pleasures around us every day that we also should be finding joy in. Opportunities for fun and meaningfulness are all around us. This is why I love this quote from Frederick Koenig: "We tend to forget that happiness doesn't come as a result of getting something we don't have, but rather of recognizing and appreciating what we do have."

7. Consciously make an effort to change your outlook.

This Frederick Koenig quote also speaks to the benefit of looking at life from a positive perspective. As hard as it is sometimes to always look at life positively, doing so will make you happier. In fact, the study I mentioned earlier from a journal of the American Psychological Association found that being positive is linked to a healthier heart, too. (University of Illinois, 2015)

8. Don't let social media make you feel bad about your own life.

Bad days happen to everyone, even if it doesn't seem that way. Social media today can sometimes make it look like everyone has a better life than you, but that's only how it seems. So, as hard as it is to do, be careful not to judge your day and your life by how it compares to someone else's.

9. Find time to volunteer or help someone else.

The sense of helping others and the world at large gives happy people what's been called a "helper's high" and seems to help protect them against feelings of anxiety and depression.

10. Discover your spiritual side.

Spirituality gives you a sense that there's something greater in the world than just you. This is a humbling way to think and seems to help happy people shrug off the not-so-great things that happen in life. Cultivating spirituality has also been shown to be good for your health. It can help reduce depression and nurture hope. (Warber et al, 2011)

11. Make a list of your blessings.

Just making it a habit to be aware of the blessings you do have on a daily basis can bring a smile to your face. Create a list if you have to, every day, of five to ten things that bring you happiness. You might just find your outlook shifting for the better.

Complementary and Alternative Therapies that Cultivate Peace

Therapies like meditation, visualization, and breathwork can all reduce anxiety and stress, improve one's outlook on life, and be a beneficial addition to a healthy lifestyle. Each works to reduce anxiety and give you an overall sense of calm. These therapies below are all ones that I use in my own life and recommend to my patients. They can help boost immune functioning and improve overall health.

Acupressure and Acupuncture

Both developed over five thousand years ago as a part of traditional Chinese medicine (also referred to as TCM). They both involve precise finger placement and pressure (acupressure) or use of needles (acupuncture) on specific body points or meridians. In Asian medical philosophy, manipulation of these points with pressure or needles can improve blood flow, healing, and tension and unblock or increase vital qi (pronounced *chee*) energy, which can not only reduce stress but can also help heal the body. It's believed that balancing the meridians allows healing energy to flow more freely in the body. (Vickers et al, 2012)

I've found that when patients have had acupuncture and acupressure, they've reported feeling better immediately afterward (they're less anxious and they sleep better) but also in the weeks following their treatment. There's a reason for this: acupressure and acupuncture are used to relieve pain and muscle tension and promote relaxation. Research published in the *Journal of the American Geriatrics Society* also showed that walking on river stone paths, which activates acupressure points on the soles of the feet, can help relieve pain, improve sleep, and improve overall physical and mental wellness in older adults. (ScienceDaily, 2005) What's more, for thousands of years, acupuncture has been used to treat disorders of the skin like eczema and psoriasis. (Pacific College, 2015)

To relieve anxiety at night and sleep better, try this acupressure tip at home: apply gentle pressure for thirty seconds to what's called the K1 point on the ball of your foot (about one-third of the way down the foot between the second and third toes, in the small indentation on the ball of the foot). Then release it for about five seconds, and press again for thirty seconds to one minute. Repeat on the other foot. (Ma et al, 2015)

Healing Touch

Healing touch, also called therapeutic touch, is a therapy that helps to restore and balance energy in the body. It was founded in 1989 by Janet Mentgen, a registered nurse. Practitioners use their hands and very light or near-the-body touch to promote relaxation and balance the energy that surrounds the body. The goal is to remove energetic blockages (similar to acupuncture or acupressure, which remove energy blockages to promote the flow of qi, to facilitate healing). There are various forms of this approach, including Reiki, energy field therapy, and therapeutic touch.

During healing touch, the practitioner focuses on areas where the energy field is determined to be stagnant or not flowing and/or on the seven main energy centers, called chakras in yoga philosophy. *Chakra* is a Sanskrit term for the energy centers that are believed to connect the physical and energetic body. Some people have referred to these chakras as our own invisible, rechargeable batteries that connect our spiritual bodies to our physical ones. (Read more about chakras on page 64.)

Healing touch has been used to help treat headaches, anxiety, and insomnia. (Klein, 2014; Keller et al, 1986; Marta et al, 2010) Many say the treatment produces a state of deep calm and relaxation. Research has shown that healing touch can also help with wound healing and decreased pain, which is why many hospitals are incorporating it into their surgery centers and cancer departments. (O'Mathuna et al, 2003)

Reiki

Reiki means universal life energy and was developed in Japan by Mikao Usui, who was inspired to devise a system of spiritual development that would be accessible to all people. He wanted a holistic system that could take the follower on a path to enlightenment without the constraints of organized religion. One of Usui's most famous quotes explains the essence of Reiki: "The Universe is me, and I am the Universe. The Universe exists in me, and I exist in the Universe. Light exists in me, and I exist in the light."

Like healing touch, Reiki healers feel the blocks in your energy and they can help rebalance this energy by using light or near-the-body touch. There is also a distant healing that can be sent. I have experienced firsthand the benefits of Reiki healing and have since been trained myself.

There are five elements of Reiki. These are:

1. The five spiritual principles or precepts

These are to be recited daily, to be followed throughout the day, or to be meditated upon:

Do not anger.

Do not worry.

Be humble.

Be honest in your work.

Be compassionate to yourself and others.

2. Breathing techniques

Breathing is so important to health and wellness. This includes diaphragmatic breathing and mindfulness breathing.

3. Hands-on palm healing

We all use our hands to heal—when we touch someone to hug or reassure them. We all give the comfort of touch. Reiki, or palm healing as it translates from the Japanese word *tenohira*, is a system of transmitting healing energy to oneself or others.

4. Symbols and mantras

A mantra, as I've mentioned earlier, is a word or sound that's repeated as a form of meditation.

5. Attunements

An attunement is a form of spiritual empowerment that passes through the teacher to the student, activating the ability to draw in more energy based on individual need. This enables them to become more effective channels for the Reiki energy.

Massage Therapy

We've probably all enjoyed a good massage at one point or another and experienced firsthand its relaxing results. I know I have. Massage is one of my go-to treats for myself when I've had a lot on my plate. There are many different types of massage therapy, from Swedish massage (designed to promote relaxation) and hot stone massage (which uses heated stones and kneading to relax muscles) to sports massage (a therapeutic massage designed to knead trouble spots). There's even facial massage to help relieve tension from the facial muscles.

The healing benefits of massage are well researched. By kneading the skin, a massage therapist is gently manipulating the muscles and soft tissue to get rid of knots in the muscles (which can develop from stress and spending too much time hunched over a computer), ultimately promoting relaxation. In doing this, massage actually causes levels of the stress hormone cortisol to decrease, which brings about immediate relaxation. It also causes the feel-good hormones serotonin and dopamine to increase, according to research published in the *International Journal of Neuroscience*. Massage has also been shown to do everything from reduce pain and speed recovery after injury to increase flexibility and boost relaxation. These are all good reasons to incorporate massage into your schedule whenever possible. (Adams et al, 2010; Caldwell, 2008; Brummitt, 2008)

I do want to add that you don't need to pay for massage to reap its benefits; self-massage also can have relaxation benefits. Rolling a tennis ball along the bottom of your bare or socked feet with firm pressure—while sitting or standing—is a form of both massage and acupressure. It works out the tense muscles in your feet but also engages relaxation pressure points on the bottom of the feet. A scalp massage is also a wonderful self-massage that you can do anytime.

Place a palm on either side of the head, bending your fingers so just your fingertips are touching the scalp. Press your fingertips into the scalp with light pressure and move them over your scalp. You can also run your fingertips lightly over your face, starting with your chin and moving your way up your cheeks and across your forehead. (Lindgren et al, 2010; Galatzer-Levy, 2014)

Osteopathy

Osteopathy is a form of medicine founded by Andrew Taylor Still in 1874 that focuses on total body, or holistic, health. This is the form of medicine that I practice. Osteopathic doctors like myself place an emphasis on self-healing and preventive medicine. We believe the body functions as an integral unit, not as a collection of separate parts.

Osteopathic physicians are also trained in osteopathic manipulative treatment or hands-on care to diagnose, treat, and prevent illness or injury. The techniques utilize stretching, gentle pressure, and resistance to help balance the body's nervous, circulatory, and lymphatic systems, thereby contributing to overall health. Some osteopaths also use very gentle movements of your skull and the bone at the bottom of the spine called the sacrum (a treatment called cranial osteopathy or craniosacral therapy).

Osteopathic manipulative treatment has been shown to relieve pain, particularly back or neck pain. Inflammatory skin diseases also get relief from osteopathic manipulation, which helps to promote lymphatic flow, thereby boosting the immune system.

The key concepts of osteopathy are:

1. The body is a unit. Each person is a unit of body, mind, and spirit.

2. The body is capable of self-regulation, self-healing, and health maintenance. When normal adaptability is disrupted, or when environmental changes overcome the body's capacity for self-maintenance, disease may develop.

3. Structure and function are linked. This is the belief that abnormal tissue structure is likely to result in disruptions in tissue function and vice versa.

Yoga

Most think of yoga as a physical activity, which it is, but it actually started in India five thousand years ago as a philosophical system to unite the body, mind, and spirit. The word *yoga* is Sanskrit for "union." It's intended to improve concentration and meditation by quieting the body, the nervous system, and the mind through the use of asanas or yoga poses and calming, diaphragmatic breathwork. It also increases muscle tone and flexibility and is a powerful stress management tool that leads to deep relaxation as well as clear-mindedness, energy, and confidence. (Hartfiel et al, 2011) (See page 113 for different types of yoga and their benefits.)

Evidence suggests that regular practice of yoga can do everything from preventing heart disease to helping symptoms of carpel tunnel syndrome, chronic back pain, insomnia, and digestive disorders like IBS. (Garfinkle et al, 1998; Tilbrook et al, 2011; Khalsa, 2004; Kuttner et al, 2006)

One aspect of yoga that's a powerful way of aligning mind, body, and spirit is using mudras or hand positions while doing poses or during meditation. How you position your hands during yoga helps to channel energy coming into, and flowing through, the body. Each finger symbolizes a different natural element: the thumb symbolizes space, the index finger symbolizes air, the middle finger symbolizes fire, the ring finger symbolizes water, and the pinky finger symbolizes the earth.

While there are hundreds of mudras, here are some of my favorite ones:

> **Gyan mudra:** This is the iconic meditation mudra with the tip of the forefinger and tip of the thumb gently touching each other. (Keep the other three fingers straight or slightly bent.) It's called the mudra of knowledge because it helps to increase concentration and focus, sharpening the memory and the mind.
>
> **Prana mudra:** Also called the mudra of life, this mudra involves touching the tips of your ring and pinky finger to the tip of your thumb. Keep the other two fingers straight or slightly bent. This mudra helps to activate energy or prana, considered the life force, in your body, reducing fatigue.
>
> **Dhyana mudra:** This mudra involves your right hand resting on top of your left palm with the tips of both thumbs touching, while resting both hands in your lap. This is the perfect mudra to do while sitting and meditating, as the right hand symbolizes enlightenment. The left hand symbolizes illusion. Doing this mudra can bring peace and tranquility.

Visualization/Guided Imagery

What you are thinking about and focusing on can manifest in your life. This is the basis of visualization and guided imagery, a meditation technique in which you close your eyes and use your imagination to create peaceful, relaxing visual images in your mind, perhaps of a goal or a dream. You can do this while relaxing and/or doing your daily breathing exercises. Often, visualization is guided, meaning someone (for example, in a relaxation, meditation, or yoga class or via an app or digital recording) helps "guide" the images you can picture in your mind.

With visualization, you can add details to your image, like color, sound, motion, and smell. You can even add a song or music. (To engage all the senses, soft music can be playing, a candle can be lit, and/or aromatherapy scents can surround you.) For example, if sitting by the ocean listening to the waves is relaxing to you, you can close your eyes and visualize sitting on the beach with the feel of the cool, wet sand between your toes. You can imagine the sound of the ocean waves hitting the shore and receding. You can envision the sound of seagulls overhead and the feel of the salty ocean mist on your skin and in your hair. While visualizing a scene like this, the entire body calms down and becomes more at peace.

The goal of visualization is to engage all the senses to make a connection between the brain and the involuntary nervous system. When the brain's visual cortex is activated without having direct input from the eyes (for instance, when we vividly picture a pleasing activity), our brain believes it is experiencing what we're visualizing, thus shifting our attention and helping clear negative thoughts. In this way, visualization can help promote relaxation and healing. Often the best time to use imagery is just before falling asleep and just after waking up.

Visualization has been shown to help lower blood pressure, reduce anxiety and depression, and help you sleep better. There are many researchers and wound care specialists who believe you can help your body heal wounds and fight disease by visualizing the anatomy or symptoms of the disease and how they are being fixed or corrected. (Papantonio, 1998) For example, if you're undergoing cancer therapy, you can imagine your immune cells fighting the cancer cells or the chemotherapy helping to eliminate the cancer cells. Taking time to focus on your body and its powerful ability to heal itself can't hurt. At best, it will relax you, which we know can boost your immune system.

When visualizing, explore not just what you want but also who you are or who you want to be. You can use the words "I am" followed by what you want to manifest into physical reality. You can use these daily too, for manifesting more than just relaxation. For example, you can repeat any of these phrases silently: *I am peaceful, I am healthy, I am beautiful, I am confident, I am strong, I am intelligent, I am successful, I am creative,* and *I am loving.* Put as much detail into the visualization as possible. Think about how you feel when you have what it is you want to manifest. Think about how it looks and feels in your hands. Envision it in detail. You are able to attract into your life all that you desire.

To get started, sit or lie down in a quiet place. Close your eyes. Take deep, regular, quiet breaths. Then begin to picture yourself in a beautiful place, real or imagined. For example, imagine that you're in a grassy field near a small running stream with a clear sky overhead. Make it as real as possible by including sounds, smells, colors, and physical sensations. You can focus on the breath, but don't make any attempt to control your breath. Focus for about five minutes.

Here are some favorite visualizations, created from the visualizations that so many people have shared with me and inspired me with over the years. The wonderful thing about visualizations is you can take inspiration from anywhere and create your own as well, depending on your own goals. (Wientjes, 2002)

Manifesting Visualization

Sit still in a quiet place. Breathe normally or gently. Breathe in through the nose and out through pursed lips. Breathe with intention.

Focus on something that has meaning to you. It could be a sound ("ahhh" for awakening of the day or light or "om" for sleep or rest), a picture, a statue, or your breath.

Envision breathing in everything that you want and breathing out that which is not holding your peace or is hurting you. Breathe out the bad memories or the hurt. Take in what you need and breathe out what is not serving your soul well.

Envision that you're breathing it out to the earth. The earth will process it, change it, and bring it back as beauty.

To remind yourself of this process, surround yourself with nature's beauty every day (e.g., a plant or cut flowers). Picture what you want.

You can do this anywhere, anytime, for what you want to see in your life. Bring what you want in the universe to you. Act as if it is already there and think of it all the time. Continually improve upon the idea. Refine it. Manifest it. Most importantly, keep it a secret. Then others' negative energies or doubts won't interrupt your goals.

Cleansing and healing visualization: Sit quietly and practice gentle, rhythmic breathing. Press your tongue against the roof of your mouth and breathe in through your nose and out through your mouth.

Picture a hunter-green-colored liquid soap and a washcloth in your hands. Take your left hand and move clockwise and your right hand and move counterclockwise, washing your body from head to toe with the washcloth and the green liquid. Picture each of your body parts inside and outside, and picture washing away any areas that are injured or in need of extra care.

If you feel like you're getting stuck in any one spot, stay in that spot and continue to wash until you get unstuck. Then let all of the unhealthy cells and green soap drain away. Release it into the ground. Then picture a bright white light. Visualize yourself washing with this healing light from head to toe, inside your body and out. Then let the white light drain out of your feet into the earth.

World peace visualization: Sit quietly in a peaceful, safe place. Be sure your phone, TV, computer, and any electronic devices are shut off. Close your eyes and take deep, rhythmic breaths in and out, in and out.

Now picture a globe of light. This globe represents the earth and the world. Feel its light, its color, and its vibration. Take a moment to revel in all that this globe is. Think about its amazing qualities, its beauty, its spiritual strength.

Now visualize a healing light enveloping this globe, with the light growing brighter and more intense. Picture harmony, well-being, and peace toward this globe. Continue to project this healing light and love onto this globe. Feel the safety and security of this healing light.

Visualize your desires for this globe: peace, love, goodness. Visualize all the people in the globe bathing in this healing light. Visualize them living in harmony and love.

Continue to visualize the globe being bathed in this light as you open your eyes and gradually become aware of your surroundings.

Take this visualization with you as you move through your daily life. Any time you hear negative news about the world, take several deep breaths and visualize this glowing light spreading healing and peace.

Meditation

This is the practice in which you can clear your mind by training it to concentrate and cut out all distractions. It helps you stop the inner chatter, which can be a source of worry, insecurity, negativity, and anger. Meditation is a method by which you can remember that you're not the voice of your mind, you're merely the one who hears it day in and day out. Through meditation, you can separate yourself from this inner chatter, a skill that will help you through many situations in life and that can bring peace. As the Hindu scripture the *Bhagavad Gita* says, "With a quiet mind, seek harmony within yourself."

The more you practice meditation, the more in control your mind will be. It will have less of a tendency to wander off in all different thought directions as it's prone to do thanks to our super busy lives. Many meditation proponents believe that meditation stimulates the transformative power of the brain and provides you with great conviction and strength to change the course of your life. This more focused approach to life manifests itself in how we act every day and how we look, too. Those of my patients who meditate regularly exude a calmer demeanor and a more radiant glow from their skin. They look and feel younger and are happier, too.

Consistent daily practice of meditation has been shown to alter our response to stress, which influences serotonin production, helping to regulate mood, sleep, and appetite. It's also been shown to boost heart health by decreasing heart and respiratory rates as well as your risk of heart attack and stroke.

If you've tried meditation and just don't love it, you may be doing the wrong kind of meditation for you. In fact, when it comes to meditation, one size or kind of meditation definitely does not fit all. Here's a guide to finding the type that's best suited to you:

1. Chakra Meditation

This is typically used when an area of your body is unhealthy, which is why it's also called healing meditation. Using specific meditations for the major chakras or energy centers in the body, you can visualize opening and cleansing these "areas" of the body. In doing so, you are also calming the body and the mind.

Root chakra (at the base of the spine) represents our foundation and plays a part in us feeling grounded. It's associated with a sense of security and basic needs like food, water, a home, and safety. Feelings of fear (i.e., fear of letting go) and worry usually signal a blockage in this chakra. This chakra is typically linked to the reproductive organs, the kidneys, the spine, and the adrenal glands. A blockage in this chakra has also been linked to lower back and leg and foot problems.

The root chakra, which is the chakra closest to the earth, corresponds with the element of the earth and the sense of smell. To enhance a root chakra meditation, you can utilize specific earth-scented and grounding essential oils like patchouli or cypress (i.e., through a diffuser). And while meditating, repeat a mantra that grounds you, such as "I am strong and I am stable" or "lam" (pronounced *laah mm*), which is the sound that vibrates with this chakra. Visualizing a lotus flower in deep red (the color of the root chakra) at the base of your spine and your pelvic floor while meditating can also help to open this chakra.

Sacral chakra (in the lower abdomen) rules our sense of abundance and well-being, as well as pleasure, emotions, and sexuality. Depression, fear of change, and sometimes even addiction issues usually indicate a blockage in this chakra. It's this chakra that's associated with the bladder, prostate, ovaries, kidneys, gallbladder, and spleen. Chronic lower back pain, constipation, urinary or kidney infections, and gynecological problems are all associated with a blocked sacral chakra.

It's the sacral chakra that corresponds with the sense of taste and the water element, which is why doing this meditation while listening to sounds of water—be it sitting near a body of water outdoors or listening to it via an app or an indoor home fountain—can help to open this chakra. Essential oils of ylang ylang or neroli can help to open this chakra during meditation. (For more information on aromatherapy, see page 59.) And while meditating, you can repeat a mantra like "I embrace life fully" or "vam" (pronounced *vaaah mmm*), which is the sound linked to the sacral chakra. Visualizing a crescent moon in orange (the color associated with this chakra) over the lower abdomen while you're meditating can also help to open this chakra.

Solar plexus chakra (in the upper abdomen) represents our ability to be self-confident and at peace with oneself. Anger and lack of direction are usually signs of a blockage in this chakra, as are overeating and excessive fatigue. This chakra is associated with the intestines and digestive function, pancreas, liver, bladder, stomach, and upper spine.

The solar plexus chakra corresponds with the sense of vision and element of fire and heat—doing this meditation while outdoors in the sun or close to a candle or fire can help to open this chakra. Using citrusy essential oils of wild orange or grapefruit while meditating can help to ground this chakra, too. And while meditating, repeat a mantra like "I am at peace with myself and my surroundings" or "ram" (pronounced *raaah mmm*), which is the sound associated with this chakra. Picturing a beautiful sunflower in vibrant yellow (the color associated with this chakra) in the upper abdomen, right above your belly button, while you're meditating can also help to open this chakra. Imagine, too, this warm yellow light spreading throughout your entire body.

Heart chakra (in the chest) rules love. It's where the physical and the spiritual parts of ourselves meet. Lack of compassion and inhumanity typically manifest when this chakra is blocked, as does anger, impatience, jealousy, and fear of betrayal. This chakra rules the heart and the lungs. Insomnia, an increase in blood pressure, and reduced immune function are usually associated with an imbalance in this chakra.

The heart chakra corresponds with the sense of touch and the element of air—why breathing in deeply and diaphragmatically during this meditation will help to open this chakra. Essential oils of rose or jasmine while meditating can help to open this chakra. And while meditating, you can repeat a mantra like "I love myself and I am open to love" or "yam" (pronounced *yaah mm*), which is the sound that activates this chakra. Picture a ball of pulsating energy in green (the color associated with this chakra) in the heart area while you're meditating to help open this chakra. Imagine, as you meditate, that this green ball is getting brighter and more vibrant and spreading throughout your entire body.

Throat chakra (in the middle of the throat) governs our ability to express ourselves. Creative blocks and problems communicating (speaking too much or inappropriately, fear of public speaking, excessive gossiping, or having trouble listening) usually indicate an imbalance with this chakra. It's this chakra that's associated with the respiratory system, the thyroid gland, and the mouth. A chronic sore throat, hoarseness, thyroid problems, and dental issues may be signs of a blocked throat chakra.

The throat chakra corresponds with the element of space and sense of hearing—using a strong ocean breath, which emits an "ocean" sound, during this meditation can help to open this area. (For steps on how to do the ocean breath, see page 113.) Calming essential oils of lavender or Roman chamomile help to ground this chakra during meditation. And while meditating, repeat a mantra like "I release the fears that block me and speak my truth with love" or "hum" (pronounced *haah mmm*), which is the sound associated with this chakra. Picturing a bright orb in crystal blue (the color associated with this chakra) in the throat area while meditating can help to remove blockages from this chakra.

Third eye chakra (between the brows) rules imagination, intuition or our "sixth sense," and wisdom. An imbalance in this chakra usually manifests with mental rigidity and a lack of foresight, inspiration, creativity, and spiritual wisdom. The eyes, brain, and pituitary gland are all ruled by this chakra. Headaches, sinus pain, fogginess or mental confusion, and eye problems are associated with a blockage in this chakra.

The third eye chakra corresponds with the sense of intuition and the element of light—why meditating near a candle can help to open this area. Utilizing essential oils of sandalwood or rosemary while meditating can help to ground this chakra too. And while meditating, repeat a mantra like "I trust my deepest wisdom and follow my life's purpose" or "sham" (pronounced *shah mmm*), which is the sound connected with this chakra. Visualizing a bright light in purple or indigo (the color associated with the third eye chakra) glowing on your forehead between your eyes and radiating light around it also helps to balance out this chakra.

Crown chakra (on the top of the head) governs inner and outer beauty, a connection to a higher consciousness, and our spirituality. Feelings of isolation, a loss of identity, closed-mindedness, and cynicism usually indicate a problem with this chakra, which is associated with the brain stem, spinal cord, and pineal gland (responsible for secreting the sleep-promoting hormone melatonin). Symptoms of a blocked crown chakra include a sensitivity to light, migraines, nervous system imbalances, ear tingling, and chronic fatigue.

The crown chakra corresponds with the sense of empathy and element of thought and universal consciousness—why meditating in a quiet, peaceful area is important while doing this meditation. Using essential oils of lime or frankincense can help to ground this chakra during meditation. And while meditating, repeat a mantra like "I am connected with the wisdom of the universe" or "om" (pronounced *aau mm*), which is the universal meditation sound that's associated specifically with this chakra. Visualizing a lotus flower with a thousand petals in bright white (the color associated with this chakra) radiating from your head while you're meditating can also help to open this chakra.

2. Heart-Centered Meditation

During this meditation, you focus on the heart area while inhaling and exhaling, a technique that helps to relax you but also brings compassion, harmony, and unconditional love into the heart to release fears and sadness and "heal" the heart.

To start, find a comfortable sitting position. Put your right hand over your heart and heart chakra. Then place your left hand over the right hand, with your thumbs touching. Take slow, deep diaphragmatic breaths in and out now and continue to breathe slowly throughout this entire meditation. Feel your heartbeat. Feel the warmth of your heart center with your hands. Continue to breathe. If your mind wanders, gently bring it back to your heart. Continue using this healing touch, but now visualize your hands sending radiant healing white light into your heart. With each breath in, keep visualizing this white light entering your heart as you recite the mantras "compassion," "healing," "harmony," and "love." Do this for five to ten minutes.

3. Mindfulness Mediation

During this meditation, you focus on the breath or a mantra without letting your mind fill up with thoughts. You can do this type of meditation anywhere (e.g., while running, horseback riding, or kayaking). It is based on the idea that you can be mindful in the moment, cutting out all other distractions, in an effort to relax and clear the mind.

You can also do this meditation while you're eating. The more mindful you are during meals, the more satisfied you'll be and the less food you'll be hungry for later on. To practice mindfulness meditation while you're eating, hold a fruit like a grape or a piece of popcorn in your hand. Think about how it looks. What is the color, size, and shape? Next, think about how it feels. Is it heavy, light, smooth, or rough? What does it smell like? Then, place the food in your mouth without chewing it. Think about how it feels. What is the texture like? Now chew it slowly. How does it feel and taste? You don't have to do each of these steps as you eat every meal, but the goal is to focus on the aspects of food as you chew and swallow, particularly how each bite tastes and feels in your mouth.

4. Transcendental Meditation

During this meditation, sit with your eyes closed and your back straight (ideally in the lotus or half lotus position) while focusing on and repeating a sound or mantra. To sit in the lotus or half lotus position, sit cross-legged with your feet placed on opposing thighs, your spine straight. (Support the knee of your top leg with a folded blanket under it if you're not able to rest it on the floor). If this position is too difficult, you can always sit in a simple cross-legged easy pose, with each foot beneath the opposite knee.

How to Meditate

While there are different types of meditation, all involve directing awareness inward by focusing on an object in the mind's eye, a mantra, or the breath. There are plenty of apps and free guided meditations (I like UCLA Mindful Awareness Center's free guided meditations; you can find them at marc.ucla.edu) that can help you learn how to quiet your mind. Follow these steps to get started:

1. *Choose a quiet place where you won't be interrupted.* Find a comfortable place to sit or lie down. If sitting, ideally you want to sit with your back straight in a lotus or half lotus posture, though this isn't necessary. Allow the tips of your thumb and index finger to touch, forming a circle. Rest the back of your hands on the lower thighs. Keep your palms open and inward to the heart in what's called the "knowledge position."

2. *Focus.* Keep your eyes open in a soft downward gaze, looking four to six feet ahead on the floor in front of you. The idea is that you're not shutting down your awareness of the space around you, but are relaxing your focus somewhat.

While meditating, if your mind begins to wander, bring it back to your breath, without judgment. Just keep practicing this. As your mind wanders, bring it back. When it wanders again, bring it back again. It's important not to repress thoughts or follow them. Just simply let them be as they are, notice them, and then return your attention to your breath. It was the Buddhist meditation master Chögyam Trungpa Rinpoche who said that when you are sitting like this, you have a flat bottom and your thoughts also have a flat bottom. Before your thoughts had little wings and were flying all around and taking you with them, but now your body is settled and your mental activity will settle down as well.

Some people find it helpful to have a mantra (a single word or sound like "ohm") or an image to focus on. Then every time your mind drifts, you simply refocus it with your mantra or visual image. Or you can just make the breath your image and your mantra. Some mantras to try:

- Om or Ohm is a classic meditation mantra that is said to contain the vibration of the sound of the universe and the beginning, middle, and end or the past, present, and future. It's a simple mantra that you can repeat at the end of each day to prepare your mind and body ready for rest.

- Om Mani Padme Hum, a Buddhist Tibetan mantra, helps to get rid of jealousy, desire, ego, and hatred. It's six syllables and each one has a meaning:

  - Om (*ohm*) destroys attachments to ego and establishes generosity.

- Ma (*mah*) removes the attachment to jealousy and establishes ethics.
- Ni (*nee*) removes the attachment to desire and establishes patience.
- Pad (*pahd*) removes the attachment to prejudice and establishes perseverance.
- Me (*meh*) removes the attachment to possessiveness and establishes concentration.
- Hum (*hum*) removes the attachment to hatred and establishes wisdom.

- Sa Ta Na Ma promotes balance for better sleep, when repeated over and over quietly before bedtime. Translated, it means "birth, life, death, rebirth."

- Har Har Makande helps remove anxiety and fear. You can repeat it before bed or before doing or encountering something that scares you. It means "the infinite creator liberates me."

- Om, Aguusti, Shina (*sha he nah*) also helps promote deep sleep. Its rhythmic sounds, repeated silently or whispered over and over, help lull you into sleep.

- Ahhh is a calming mantra. While saying it, visualize a pleasant and productive day. You can use this to visualize how you want your own day to begin or just repeat it quietly when you're trying to relax. The "ahhh" mantra is also considered to be the sound of the heart chakra and is associated with love and compassion for yourself and for others.

3. *Try to meditate five minutes a day.* Then slowly work up to fifteen to thirty minutes once or twice a day. If you can't

fit in a complete session, try to fit in a few minutes. To help you, set a meditation timer, which can use the sound of a relaxing chime or Tibetan singing bowls. Many are available today as apps for your phone. This way, you won't have to be constantly looking at the clock to figure out how much longer you have to meditate. One I like is the free *Insight Meditation Timer*, available on most devices.

Keep in mind that, as with learning any new skill, practice is key. Being able to push aside all the thoughts in your brain to focus on your breath *will* become a little easier each time you do it.

Meditations for Modern Life

Try one or all of these meditations, adapting them to you and what you want and need. Remember, meditations are intensely personal. There is no right or wrong way to do them. The most important part of meditation is taking deep, relaxing breaths and focusing your thoughts, allowing other thoughts to pass gently from the mind.

1. Healthy Relationships Meditation: "I Am Open to Attracting Love"

This meditation connects you to your heart space, opening it up to attract love for both yourself and others. The more you practice this, the more you'll attract love into your life. As an option, you can do this meditation holding a rose quartz crystal in one or in both palms, which helps realign the heart chakra (see more about crystals later in this chapter).

Lie in a comfortable shavasana or corpse yoga pose position, with your heels spread wide, arms a few inches from the body with palms facing upward. (When palms are facing upward, it positions you in an open receiving mode.)

Close your eyes and allow yourself to relax. Take deep, gentle breaths in and out. Picture yourself in the most beautiful garden, a garden of love. See the beautiful flowers. Smell the sweet scents. Bathe in the golden sunlight.

Start to consciously relax the muscles in your body, starting with your facial muscles, down to your neck muscles, into your chest muscles, and all the way to your toes. As you do this, spread the warm golden loving sunlight from the garden through each part of your body.

Bathe in the warmth of this golden light. Feel its heat, revel in its radiance. Allow other thoughts that come in your mind to pass gently, without judgment. Continue to take your deep, rhythmic, relaxing breaths.

Now visualize your heart. Consciously open the blinds of your heart and let in this golden sunlight from the garden of love. Revel in the warmth of this light as it bathes your heart, as your heart becomes ripe for love. Open your heart to pure overflowing love.

Repeat (silently to yourself or out loud) this mantra: Love is in me. I am worthy of love.

Now say goodbye to this beautiful sunlit garden, but know that you can come back any time to feed your heart, to grow in love. Gradually open your eyes and lie quietly, listening to your rhythmic breathing. Stretch your arms and legs, doing whatever feels comfortable to you. Slowly get up. And remember, you are blessed with love.

2. Prosperity Meditation: "I Want to Attract Abundance into My Life"

This meditation opens your mind and spirit to having prosperity and wealth. As motivational speaker and author Wayne Dyer once said, "Abundance is not something we acquire. It's something we tune in to."

Sit quietly and comfortably. Close your eyes. Place your palms face up on your legs, ready to receive abundance. Take gentle, rhythmic breaths in and out. As you breathe in, visualize the prosperity and abundance that you are welcoming into your life. Visualize, in vivid detail, the things you are now ready to receive with open arms. (Setting an intention of what you want in life helps to focus your energy on receiving this.)

Allow negative thoughts and habits regarding money, wealth, and abundance to flow out of your body with each breath out. Continue to do this, allowing negative energy and fears to enter and leave your consciousness, without judgment.

As you breathe in and out, repeat this mantra: I attract wealth and prosperity with every breath I take.

Allow yourself to breathe in and out rhythmically for several more breaths before opening your eyes and returning your focus to the world around you.

3. Healing Meditation: "I Am Strong, I Am Healthy"

This meditation helps guide healing in the body, both physically and emotionally. It can be done any time—while at home or at work or waiting in a doctor's office.

Sit or lie in a comfortable position. Close your eyes. Breathe gently in and out.

Give your entire body permission to relax, to just be for a while. Relax beginning with the muscles in your head and face, move down to your neck and then to your shoulders. Feel the breaths in your lungs as you relax your chest muscles. Take a moment to appreciate your body working for you—your lungs, your heart, your body working in tandem to keep you strong.

Now relax your arms, your hands, your abdomen, your back, your legs, and your feet. Continue to breathe gently in and out.

Focus on your heart beating. Appreciate the strength of your heart and everything it does for you.

Now visualize a bright white light in the form of a ball. As you breathe in, visualize this light spreading into your body, cleansing your body and your mind. Experience this light going through every part of your body, working to cleanse, purify, rejuvenate, and balance your whole being. Have this light concentrate on any areas that need extra healing. Envelop those areas with this white light.

Feel the light healing your body and your emotions. Now as you breathe out, consciously release negative energy from your body and mind.

As you are breathing in this light, repeat this mantra: "I am strong. I am healthy."

Continue to bathe in the light, taking deep, relaxing breaths. As you breathe in, visualize more light infusing your body. As you breathe out, visualize negative energy leaving your body.

Gently open your eyes when you're ready and slowly become aware of everything around you. Give yourself time before you get up and get back into your life.

4. Shower Meditation: "I Attract Positivity"

This meditation helps you rid yourself of negative thoughts and energy and helps you jump-start healthier habits and attitudes. You can do this quick meditation in the shower every morning if you have time.

Close your eyes. Feel the water running from your head to your toes. Become aware of this sensation and how the water feels as it hits every part of your body. Allow your mind to quiet as you focus on the sound and feel of the running water. Slowly breathe in and out for the count of ten breaths.

As the water runs down your body into the drain, visualize that it takes with it all the negativity in your life. Picture the water forming a glowing protective ring around your body, shielding you from negativity and stress.

Gently open your eyes and resume your shower or get out and dry off.

5. Commuting Meditation: "I Love What I Do"

This meditation helps reduce work stress and frustration and makes room for creativity and inspiration. Try this on your commute to work.

Relax your shoulders and sit comfortably in your seat. Keep your eyes open, with your hands on the wheel if you're driving and stuck in traffic. Take deep rhythmic breaths in and out for the count of ten.

Bring your awareness to what or who is causing your stress and creativity block. Be aware of how it makes you feel.

Say this mantra quietly or internally to this feeling: "I love what I do. I am good at what I do. I choose to see this situation [or person] differently from this point on."

As you exhale, visualize the negativity and frustration and stress leaving your body. As you inhale, visualize positivity and inspiration filling your body and mind. Continue to do this for ten breaths in and out or until you're out of traffic.

6. Everyday Meditation: "My Life Is Filled with Happiness and Gratitude"

This meditation helps bring light when your world seems filled with darkness and despair. Both Buddhism and Taoism teach this as the inner smile meditation.

Sit on a chair or lie comfortably on the floor. Rest your right hand on top of your left palm, in your lap, with the tips of both thumbs touching. Close your eyes and breathe rhythmically in and out for the count of ten.

Let your jaw relax and smile as you would smile to another person. Let the smile fill your face. If your smile fades, just continue to bring it back without judgment while you continue to breathe.

Visualize what you have to be grateful for. Gently push aside the negative thoughts that make their way into your mind and insert happy thoughts. Continue to smile while breathing in and out. Then after each breath in, repeat this mantra: "I choose to be happy. Life is good."

Then slowly exhale. After ten breaths, allow yourself to open your eyes and smile for yourself and the world.

7. Bedtime Meditation: "I Will Get Restful Sleep"

This meditation helps improve insomnia and quality of sleep. You can listen to soft sleep-inducing music without words, too, as long as you're not gazing at a computer or phone screen while you're listening.

To do this meditation, simply lie on your back or side, whichever is more comfortable for you. Take ten deep, slow breaths in and out.

Let your mind wander at first and then slowly bring your mind to this mantra, which you will repeat over and over: "Om, agasti (*ah-gah-sti*) shahina (*sha-he-nah*)."

Focus on the slow hypnotic rhythm of your breath in and out along with this mantra, "om, ah gah sti, sha he nah." As worries or anxious thoughts enter your mind, let them gently float away on a fluffy white cloud.

Continue to breathe and focus on your mantra until you drift off to sleep.

Aromatherapy

Aromatic plants have been used in healing for millennia, and essential oils have been used since the Middle Ages. Modern aromatherapy was founded, and the term was coined, in the 1920s by French chemist René-Maurice Gattefossé. After burning his hand in a lab explosion, he put the burned skin in a bowl of lavender oil and was surprised to find that his burns healed quickly without infection, pain, or scarring. He then started investigating essential oils for treating various skin conditions. He studied oils from flowers, leaves, fruits, barks, and roots and how they affected physical and mental health.

In France and Japan, medical aromatherapy is an established and accepted field. The theory behind it is that when we breathe in certain scents through the nose, these scents send chemical messages through nerves to the brain, triggering emotional and physiological effects that can influence the immune, circulatory, and respiratory systems. Science aside, I can speak firsthand to the benefits of aromatherapy: the scents of lavender and ylang ylang essential oils definitely help me feel more relaxed.

There are plenty of options for using essential oils: apply lotions or creams with essential oils in them; rub roller balls filled with essential oils on the wrists, temples, base of the neck, or behind the ears; and use them in diffusers, which infuse the air around you with scent. A few words of caution about essential oils, however: essential oils should never be applied directly to the skin, especially if you have sensitive skin, as they can trigger irritation. They should always be diluted first with what's called a carrier oil (examples include fractionated coconut oil, sweet almond oil, grapeseed oil, and jojoba oil).

Crystal Therapy

Crystals, minerals, and gems have been used for thousands of years to bring about emotional and physical balance. References to crystals date back to the ancient Sumerians and ancient Egyptians. Crystals, known for their religious connotations, have also played a part in all religions throughout history, with people reaching for crystals to help bring about spiritual wellness and balance. Today, crystals (a word that means "frozen light") are used for meditation and during Reiki, and to help focus or concentrate energies.

While there is no concrete evidence or research pointing to the benefits of crystals, there is plenty of anecdotal evidence from those who speak about the power of crystals. I myself am instinctively drawn to crystals, particularly while doing Reiki and meditation. My belief: if you believe in the energy of crystals, they can help in your own life.

Here's how they're thought to work: we know that our bodies are energetic and that we each vibrate an energy and emit energy. The universe vibrates energy too, and our thoughts create vibrations in the universe. Using semi-precious stones from the earth, proponents of crystal therapy employ the healing powers of crystals. By opening your heart and mind to crystals, you're becoming in tune with their energy and connection with the healing powers of the earth. Bottom line: If you're drawn to crystals and believe in their energy, this positive energy can help in your own life.

There's something to be said for the idea that crystals help to focus our energies and our intentions. In fact, setting intentions while using crystals helps to amplify these goals. To set an intention, close your eyes and allow your breath to slow and become relaxed. Clear your mind of any daily stresses and think of things that make you happy. State aloud what you want your crystal to help you with (for example, "I want to be free from the negative energy of other people" or "I want to strive to be my happiest, most loving self").

How to Cleanse and Energize with Crystals

Experts in crystals say the stones choose you instead of you choosing the stones. To pick one, hold it while you're feeling calm, and see how it makes you feel. Does it make you feel energized or depleted? Are you calm while holding the stone or are you agitated? Pay attention to your feelings and use these feelings to guide your choice of crystal. It's important, too, to energize a crystal before using it. To do this, you can hold it under water, set it with a cleansing stone like quartz, or place it in sunlight or moonlight. You can also use sound vibrations: place it in the center of a Tibetan singing bowl, tap the bowl with the wooden mallet while holding it gently or while it sits on a pillow, then circle the bowl with the mallet, allowing the vibrations to cleanse the crystal.

Some of the most popular crystals include:

- Agate: helps increase self confidence
- Amethyst: relieves stress and brings balance back into your life, making it a perfect stone for meditation
- Angelite: helps with happy, soothing sleep
- Amazonite: soothing; helps to decrease irritation
- Aventurine: helps increase abundance
- Black tourmaline: helps you get rid of bad habits; it also helps protect you from the negative energy of others
- Blue calcite: calming; it helps boost powers of communication
- Blue celestite: brings tranquility and harmony to your space and your spirit; it's also referred to as a "cosmic lullaby"
- Brown calcite: grounding; it boosts feelings of security
- Carnelian: helps to inspire creativity
- Citrine (natural): helps bring abundance to your life; it helps create a positive outlook
- Clear quartz: amplifies your intentions; this stone also helps to cleanse the energy from other crystals
- Fluorite: helps clear mental and emotional confusion, making it a perfect stone to have while meditating
- Garnet: helps improve health; it grounds you

- Green calcite: improves finances
- Green aventurine: cleanses negativity, promotes harmony and balance, encourages good luck and prosperity
- Halite: encourages self-love; it lifts depression
- Hematite: helps ground you and reconnects you with the earth
- Kyanite: helps to balance the chakras
- Labradorite: encourages self-awareness, heightens intuition and consciousness; it keeps physical, mental, and spiritual aspects in balance
- Lepidolite: imparts a sense of calm during stressful times; it balances mind and spirit
- Malachite: inspires courage for risk taking and change
- Moonstone: helps balance out emotions
- Orange calcite: boosts passion and joy
- Red jasper: helps ground you spiritually; it encourages emotional balance
- Rose quartz: realigns the heart chakra, opening you up to self-love and the love of others; this crystal is good to have in the bedroom
- Selenite: helps cleanse negative energy from the body; it's good to place by your bed to help you sleep at night
- Sodalite: strengthens your inner sixth sense or intuition; it helps release tension and fears
- Shungite: protects from dangerous energy, which is why some keep one near their cell phone, computer, and Wi-Fi to protect from harmful radiation

• Turquoise: helps ward off negativity and strengthen love and friendship bonds; it's a healing stone

Chakras and Crystals

You can place crystals on one or more of your seven chakras or spiritual energy centers to help you help tap in to your body's vibrational energy and amplify what you want. Prana or chi flows throughout these chakras, which, as I mentioned earlier, correspond with specific organs and systems in the body. When any of these energy centers are blocked (see below), certain symptoms can manifest themselves.

• Root chakra: A red jasper crystal can be placed on the root chakra for grounding.

• Sacral chakra: A carnelian crystal can be placed on the sacral chakra to enhance peace and self-confidence.

• Solar plexus chakra: A citrine crystal can be placed on the solar plexus chakra to dissipate negative energy.

• Heart chakra: A green aventurine crystal can be placed on the heart chakra to align physical, mental, and emotional well-being.

• Throat chakra: A sodalite crystal can be placed on the throat chakra to enhance group communication.

• Third eye chakra: An amethyst crystal can be placed on the third eye chakra to encourage spirituality.

• Crown chakra: A clear quartz crystal can be placed on the crown chakra to clear away negative energy and to provide clarity of consciousness.

Using Crystals in Your Home or Office

Feng shui, the art of arranging and designing your home or work space to promote healing and balance, uses crystals to help focus the energy of a space. I use crystals both at home and in my office. In fact, my staff knows how much I love crystals, so they bought me a labradorite crystal last year for my birthday. I keep it in my office, as it helps keep physical, mental, and spiritual aspects in balance. Here are some crystal uses in your home and work spaces.

To protect your space: Black tourmaline placed by the front door or office door helps to absorb negative energy.

To stay energized: Place quartz crystals at work or at home to help bring clarity of mind, so you can stay focused. They can also boost energy while simultaneously clearing the energy of your space.

For better sleep: There are plenty of crystals that can help promote good energy in your bedroom, such as angelite for happy dreams and lepidolite for enhancing restful sleep. Place them on your bedside table or under your pillow.

For healthier relationships: A bowl of rose quartz crystals placed in the bedroom or near your bedside helps promote love.

To attract wealth: Place citrine in your work areas at home and in your office to attract prosperity.

To relieve stress and promote peace: Place the blue celestite crystal on the areas of your body feeling tension and stress, while you take deep relaxation breaths.

Herbal Medicine

Herbal medicine relies on plants or plant extracts—which are rich in a variety of natural chemical compounds—as treatments. It's been used since ancient times in many different cultures throughout the world as a way of keeping the body healthy and treating illness.

I am a big fan of using fresh and dried herbs while cooking. Some of my favorites include parsley, garlic, chives, rosemary, basil, thyme, dill, turmeric, and oregano. (See some of the recipes I use these herbs in the Healthy Mediterranean Recipes section on page 183.) They're rich in antioxidants and have so many health-promoting benefits. When we use cooking herbs and spices that have disease-preventing effects, for example, we're taking advantage of herbal health benefits. When using herbs, fresh or dried is always best. Here are some of the top health-promoting herbs and their benefits:

- Aloe reduces redness/swelling from burns and skin inflammation; it also calms skin.
- Arnica helps reduce bruising and swelling.
- Basil is an anti-inflammatory and antibacterial that may also fight viruses.
- Cilantro/coriander is a natural preservative/antibacterial that aids in detoxification.
- Cinnamon is an antifungal that also may help those with diabetes. Cinnamaldehyde, the compound that gives cinnamon its distinctive flavor and smell, is a powerful immune booster.
- Dill is an antibacterial that aids in digestion and is a breath freshener.

- Garlic is a powerful anti-inflammatory and immune booster.
- Ginger helps aid indigestion and nausea.
- Mint is a natural decongestant that also soothes indigestion; it calms and cools the skin in the case of insect bites, rashes, and other irritations.
- Oregano is a powerful antibacterial and anti-inflammatory.
- Parsley supports kidney function (and natural detoxification) and is an anti-inflammatory.
- Rosemary is a potent anti-inflammatory and may help keep eyesight sharp.
- Thyme is an antimicrobial and antibacterial that helps treat acne and skin fungal infections, and protects against food-borne infections.
- Turmeric/curcumin is a powerful anti-inflammatory and may help boost memory.

Music/Art Therapy

Indulging in creative pursuits like art, music, and dance is incredibly de-stressing. I know firsthand that they offer an outlet for expression and for our souls to speak, taking us out of the stresses of day-to-day life. This has been shown in healthcare centers that offer creative expression classes to patients and to caregivers as a way to express what they're going through in a different way. Positive imagery and expression, through creative pursuits, can also benefit the viewer or listener. Research shows, for example, that calming, peaceful artwork in hospitals can help encourage a patient's healing process, while the opposite—stark, depressing walls and even the wrong kind of art, like disturbing pictures—can cause physical distress and even hinder healing. There is also some evidence that art can help reduce hospital stays, too. Other studies show that art can help with quality of life for those suffering from Alzheimer's disease.

Music, in particular, has incredible healing powers, something that so many of us already instinctively know from just listening to music and seeing the relaxing effect it has on us. Music as a healing influence has also been documented as far back as the time of Aristotle and Plato. The idea of music as therapy has been used to help the physical, emotional, cognitive, and social needs of individuals.

Modern-day music therapists work in hospitals, rehabilitative facilities, senior centers and nursing homes, and schools because the benefits of music have been widely documented in research. Some of the well-documented ways music therapy has been used are to alleviate surgical pain in conjunction with anesthesia or pain medication; to elevate patients' mood and counteract depression; to promote movement for physical rehabilitation; to calm or sedate, often to induce sleep; to counteract apprehension or fear; and to lessen muscle tension for the purpose of relaxation. Music therapy is also used with the elderly to increase or maintain their level of physical, mental, and social/emotional functioning. The sensory and intellectual stimulation of music can help maintain a person's quality of life. (Eureka Alert, 2015)

One study, conducted by researchers in China, used soothing music with patients undergoing thoracic surgery. It found that listening to just thirty minutes of soft music a day for three days helped these patients experience less postoperative pain and anxiety. Not to mention these patients also had lower blood pressure and heart rates. This finding was backed up by a comprehensive review of studies on the topic, conducted by British researchers, which found that patients who listen to music before, during, and after surgery had less pain and anxiety overall and had less need for pain medication. (Liu et al, 2015)

There's also something called ambient music, which is a genre of music that puts an emphasis on tone and atmosphere over traditional musical rhythm, melody, composition, and words. It's a form of slow instrumental music with repetitive, soothing sound patterns to generate a sense of calmness. Nature soundscapes are typically included in ambient music, along with sounds from the synthesizer, piano, strings, and flute. Drumming is also tremendously hypnotic and rhythmic and has the power to relax you. (Lies et al, 2015)

The power of music was something that I discovered firsthand when I was in junior high. My science class assignment was to write and perform an at-home experiment that could be measured somehow. I remember cooking with my grandmother on the Saturday afternoon after I was given my homework and thinking about what I wanted to measure. I knew that I had to keep it within a low budget, but I also wanted an "A."

My grandmother and I were making an avocado salad at the time and it hit me: I would measure whether an avocado plant would grow any differently whether exposed to music or not. I loved listening to music then—and still do today—and intuitively, even at that young age, knew that music would probably make a difference in a plant's growth. My grandmother gave me two pits from the avocados we were using for our salad, and I soaked them in water so they could take root.

When they had rooted, I planted them in soil. I positioned both plants in front of a window, on the same side of the house but in different rooms. One plant had constant low-level music playing next to it and the other didn't. I then spent the next several weeks watering them with the same amount of water, carefully measuring their growth, and charting my results. As expected, the plant that was exposed to music grew significantly larger. (And yes, I did get an "A" on the assignment, which made me so happy and proud and planted the "seeds" for a career in holistic health and wellness!)

Nature Therapy

Plenty of research shows that being outdoors with fresh air, trees, and elements of nature including birds and wildlife helps to relax us and keep us healthy by reducing blood pressure, heart rate, muscle tension, and stress. In fact, sometimes there's nothing that I love more than taking a meditative walk in the park in my free time. It's mind clearing and incredibly calming.

Japanese researchers have shown that spending a short time in nature, called "forest bathing," actually boosts the activity of immune cells, which help to fight illness and disease, for up to seven days. Other researchers from around the world have shown that walking outdoors among trees and wildlife boosts energy as well as creativity. (Morimoto et al, 2007)

Numerous studies have shown the stress-reducing benefits of being surrounded by nature. One study, published in the journal *Proceedings of the National Academy of Science*, found that walking for just ninety minutes in nature actually reduced activity in an area of the brain called the subgenual prefrontal cortex, which is associated with anxiety and depression. Another Australian study found that taking regular forty-second "micro breaks" throughout the day to look at nature or even pictures of nature helps to reduce stress and mental fatigue. (Ryan et al, 2010; Jordan, 2015)

Nature can also boost a patient's recovery and reduce pain. One study conducted at Texas A & M University found that patients who had a view of trees outside their hospital rooms actually healed faster and had less pain than those patients whose windows looked out at a wall. (Gardner, 2015; Clay, 2001)

Everyday Enlightenment

Chronic stress can result in a disconnected body, mind, and spirit. But these parts need to be in sync for true health and beauty. In the words of the Greek philosopher Plato, "The cure of the part should not be attempted without treatment of the whole. No attempt should be made to cure the body without the soul … This is the great error of our day, that physicians first separate the soul from the body."

This is why, whenever my patients come into my office, I offer them much more than just skincare advice. I talk to them about their lives, too, and as a result, they tell me they leave feeling better about themselves. I'm a big believer that confidence and happiness in one's life, along with strong self-esteem, contributes to great skin and a healthy body as well.

Here's the key: it's often the simplest gestures every day that can make us feel better, boost our mood, and calm us, reducing stress and boosting health, including the health of our skin. Call it everyday spiritual enlightenment. These are the simple reminders that I give to my patients and are good bits of advice for everyone.

> **Take your vacation days.** You've earned them. Don't wait for the right moment. How many of us wait for enough money or the exact right time to take a vacation or do something that we love? So many unused vacation days go to waste for so many Americans. Don't wait. Schedule that time off or visit that place you've always wanted to see.

> **Re-frame your mindset.** We all have an underlying pattern of thoughts that plays over and over in our minds. Become aware of them and direct them in a more positive way. If you ruminate on the last thing that bothered you, it can ruin your

day, but stopping that repetitive pattern of thoughts in its tracks can help you to move on without added stress. This is something that becomes easier once you spend time in quiet thought and/or meditation. There will be things that happen that challenge you, but decide to keep a good attitude regardless of what happens. In fact, just trying to be happy has been shown to make you more positive overall. And as Lao Tzu has said, "If you correct your mind, the rest of your life will fall into place."

Change the lens through which you see the world and other people. Sometimes it's easy to get stuck with thought patterns that are critical of others. But by being accepting of others' differences, you can achieve inner peace. Similar to when the mind wanders off during meditation and you bring it back to your mantras, you have to keep bringing your mind back to acceptance of others when you want to be critical. And if there are toxic people in your life who are creating stress and anxiety and affecting your health and well-being, it may be time to walk away from them or at least limit the time you spend with them.

Pay attention to your inner GPS. Listen to how you feel (a.k.a. your gut response or intuition) and act on it. Your mind can lie but your feelings and emotions won't. They are aligning you with your true path, your inner self. I liken the gut to our own inner GPS. The intuitive mind has often been called "a sacred gift" and the rational mind "a faithful servant." But in our society today, we honor the servant and have forgotten the gift. Follow your dreams or inner thoughts and desires. Follow the calling you feel deep within you.

Take time out of every day to nourish your spiritual self. Set aside time every day to connect to your higher self with moments of silence. This could be while you're outdoors walking, at your desk, or while meditating.

Don't get stuck in a negativity rut. Life is easier if you accept the things that happen for what they are and move on. Try not to hold on to the negative (thoughts and criticisms) but let it pass by or through you. Letting go also helps free up that energy that you're devoting to the negativity. Think of yourself standing in the middle of a shallow, moving river. You're there to experience the river but not to try to stop it or control the flow. In the words of one anonymous quote, *"Happiness can only exist in acceptance."* Enjoy life; accept what happens and the things that you cannot change. Don't try to resist or fight it and you'll find that you're more peaceful and more resilient with anything life sends your way.

Realize that good often comes out of bad experiences. The things that we learn through our experiences, both good and bad, help to better us, make us grow, and even empower us. The next time you experience something that you feel is bad, look deeper into it to find the lesson or positive that came from it. It may take some time but eventually you'll be able to find something positive that you can learn from and even use to help others.

Incorporate mindfulness into the everyday. Be in the moment while trying to block out thoughts of tomorrow or next week. Life is now. As Albert Einstein once said, "I never think of the future; it comes soon enough."

Take thirty seconds every day to give thanks. Be thankful to be alive, for family, for friends, for health, for a good deed from a stranger. Taking a moment every day for thanks is critical to overall happiness.

Resent less. Forgiveness, as many researchers have found, is also good for your health, sleep quality, blood pressure, heart rate (and your heart health), anxiety levels, rates of depression, stress, and even cholesterol levels. Do your health a favor—add more peace to your life, and forgive. (Westervelt, 2012)

Don't only focus on your outer purpose or goal (for instance, career or riches) but also on each step of the way and how you build your inner purpose and consciousness. Your journey in life has both an outer purpose (to reach a goal or accomplish something) and an inner purpose (this is the journey into yourself) and they're intricately entwined and both essential to your overall health and beauty. In fact, having a purpose in life motivates a person to optimize their health, which means they're more likely to take care of themselves.

Show kindness, compassion, and generosity to others. It's contagious and just feels good. It may also be hardwired in our brains to be giving. Neuroscientists at the National Institutes of Health found that we have circuits in our brains that regulate empathy and the desire to help others. What's more, the areas of the brain involved give off a pleasurable response, as well as producing brain chemicals like oxytocin, the hormone that promotes social bonding, and dopamine, the pleasure chemical, once we act on our altruistic impulses.

Believe that you have something to offer this world. It's important to believe in yourself, love yourself, and fulfill your innermost dreams, no matter what other people say or who does or doesn't believe in you. By following your heart you're staying aligned with your higher self. Work toward the goals that *you* want to achieve. Doing so will boost happiness and health.

Where do you go from here? Consider something called *ojas* (pronounced *oh-jus*) from Ayurvedic medicine as your ultimate goal. Ayurveda is a holistic healing system that originated in India over five thousand years ago. Pure beauty, according to ayurveda, is clear, glowing skin, silky hair, happy eyes, youthfulness, and even a pleasant smell. This is the result of inner and outer happiness and health, and ayurveda sums it up as ojas. Ojas is referred to in ayurveda as the sap of life. True inner and outer beauty and health that radiates from a relaxed, peaceful state. This state of balance is a result of finding peace in your life, but it's also a result of proper diet, exercise, and sleep. And that's what I want to talk about in the coming chapters: the things you need, how to incorporate them into a busy life, and why it's so important to this cultivation of the ojas, for longevity and true inner and outer beauty.

CHAPTER 3

GIVE YOUR DIET A MEDITERRANEAN MAKEOVER

ONE OF MY PATIENTS, Samantha, has been troubled by adult acne for years. She came to see me because she had tried other treatments that just weren't bringing her long-term relief. We talked about the treatments that were right for her, such as topical acne medications, but we also addressed some critical aspects to healthy skin, including her diet and her lifestyle.

Samantha changed her diet, cutting down on soda and fast food and opting for nutrient-rich whole foods instead of take-out. Samantha also started taking Vinyasa yoga and meditating to reduce her stress, and swapped out her makeup and moisturizer for non-comedogenic or non-pore-clogging options.

The result: Samantha's skin cleared up and stayed acne-free. She developed a healthy glow and began to look years younger. She recently told me that she feels like a new person and gets compliments all the time on how great she looks. "At my age," she told me, "my skin has never looked better!"

Like Samantha, patient after patient in my practice tells me that when they follow my advice about topical treatments, eating a healthy diet, and making healthy life choices, their skin is transformed. I remind patients to treat their skin as one very important part of their whole being. As I've discussed earlier, every aspect of your body and spirit, including your spirituality, works together. When one part of the body is out of balance, it shows up on the skin. And then, when the body is out of balance for long periods of time, whole-body illness and disease sets in and eventually your longevity is affected.

Consider it this way: the skin, one of the largest organs of the body, is a very important part of your whole body. In fact, problems on the skin can be the very first sign that something's out of balance with the rest of your body.

This is why, when it comes to diet, I recommend a Mediterranean style of eating, which is healthy and delicious. The benefits of this diet have been proven over hundreds of years and go way beyond the skin, feeding what I like to say is truly beauty and health from the inside out.

What Is the Mediterranean Diet?

We've all heard the term "Mediterranean diet," but it's actually not a specific diet plan or miracle cleanse that will help you magically drop pounds. It's more of a collection of eating habits or a style of eating that's followed by the countries bordering the Mediterranean Sea, including Greece, southern Italy, and Spain. (It's also very similar to the modern-day DASH diet, which stands for Dietary Approaches to Stopping Hypertension.)

The Mediterranean diet is high in olive oil, fish, legumes, fresh fruit (typically as a daily dessert), nuts, unrefined cereals, and fresh vegetables, along with a moderate consumption of dairy (mostly as cheese and yogurt) and poultry and limited amounts of red meat. Because of this way of eating, it's also a diet low in bad saturated fat and high in good, monounsaturated and polyunsaturated fat, as well as dietary fiber.

A Mediterranean diet is fresh and filled with what I like to call longevity food and nutrients, key nutrients that keep your body humming along at its healthiest and your skin at its radiant best. (For some of my favorite recipes that incorporate these ingredients, see "Healthy Mediterranean Recipes" in the appendix, page 183.) More specifically, it involves eating two to three servings of fresh fish a week, plenty of whole grains like barley, bulgur wheat, and steel-cut oats, and colorful fruits and vegetables. Color-dense fruits and vegetables, like red grapes, green kiwi, and purple and orange sweet potatoes are rich in a variety of nutrients including key health-promoting antioxidants like flavonoids, carotenoids, vitamin E, and lycopene.

Mediterranean people also take time to relax and enjoy their meals with others, an important health-promoting social aspect. Socializing, as one study in the *American Journal of Public Health* showed, is important for maintaining good mental health and warding off diseases like dementia, Alzheimer's, and even heart disease. Socializing also promotes happiness, a key factor for inner and outer beauty.

The Many Benefits of a Mediterranean Diet
If you make at least half your plate fruits and vegetables, you'll get as many good-for-you (and good-for-your-skin) nutrients as possible.

There are a lot of things my patients notice when switching over to this type of diet: more energy, less sickness, weight loss, better sleep, and healthier, more radiant skin. It's no wonder then that the Greek island of Ikaria has been called "the island where people forget to die." It's here where Ikarian men are nearly four times as likely as their American counterparts to reach the age of ninety. They also live about eight to ten years longer before succumbing to cancers and cardiovascular disease and they suffer less depression and about a quarter the rate of dementia. These long-living, healthy Ikarians eat a Mediterranean diet, consuming about six times as many beans a day as Americans, eating fish twice a week and meat four to five times a month (typically from their own livestock), and eating much less refined sugar. These island people also consume high levels of olive oil and antioxidant-rich wild greens from their own gardens. Followers of this diet limit the kinds of foods common in an American diet: red meat, butter, stick margarine, cheese, pastries/sweets, and fried and fast food.

This type of vegetable-based diet contributes to not just how long you live, but the vitality in those years. It helps keep you happy, radiant, energetic, and mobile, without aches and pains. It has also been shown to have numerous health benefits.

- *It keeps your heart healthy.* In a Harvard School of Public Health study conducted with young midwestern firefighters, researchers found that the firefighters who ate this type of diet high in polyunsaturated fats, which come from fish and plants, had lower risk factors for cardiovascular disease. In fact, in a separate study, Greek researchers found that people who followed a Mediterranean diet were 47 percent less likely to develop heart disease over a ten-year period than those who didn't follow the diet. They were also less likely to gain weight, which is a risk factor for heart disease. (American College of Cardiology, 2015)

- *It keeps your brain sharp.* Eating a Mediterranean-style diet helps prevent your mind from deteriorating as it does with dementia and Alzheimer's. In fact, in one study published in the *Journal of the American Medical Association*, this style of healthy eating was found to reduce the risk of developing Alzheimer's by 48 percent. (Scarmeas et al, 2009)

- *It reduces your risk of cancer.* Eating this way has been shown to reduce your risk of cancer, from stomach cancer to breast cancer and endometrial cancer. This plant-heavy style of eating may also protect against skin cancer. Mediterranean populations have very low rates of skin cancer despite living in sunny climates. Israeli researchers theorize that the components of a Mediterranean diet, and namely the powerful disease-fighting antioxidants found in it, may provide protection against skin cancer.

- *It reduces your risk of diabetes.* Eating a plant-rich diet can help improve insulin sensitivity. According to researchers at the Harvard School of Public Health, 90 percent of type 2 diabetes can be avoided by eating a Mediterranean-style diet, getting regular physical activity, and not smoking. (Martinez-Gonzalez et al, 2008)

- *It reduces your risk of developing depression.* Spanish researchers at the University of Navarra found that people who follow a Mediterranean-style of eating, specifically getting enough fruits, nuts, vegetables, legumes, healthy grains, and fish, are less likely to develop depression.

How a Mediterranean Diet
Translates to Modern Life

If you look at the diet of Mediterranean populations, it's easy to see that food is where everything begins. It nourishes us, provides us energy, makes us healthy or establishes the groundwork for illness and disease, gives a glow or dull cast to our skin, and can prolong our lives or shorten them. (Buettner, 2012)

We know inherently what's good for us and what we *should* be eating: more fruits and vegetables, healthy whole grains, protein, healthy fats (as compared with the unhealthy fried ones), low sugar and sodium, fewer unhealthy carbohydrates, plenty of water not soda, and no junk. But as much as we *know* about good nutrition, it's so very complicated and hard to put this healthy way of eating into practice in our modern society. Long work days, after-school and weekend children's activities, lack of time to prepare healthy foods, the 24/7 availability of unhealthy convenience foods, and few to no backyard gardens all factor into why eating a healthy diet isn't so easy to implement in our daily lives. But food is the foundation for true health and beauty. (Crooks et al, 2008)

How Food Affects Our Bodies and Our Health

I want to share the story of my grandmother. When I was young, she was overweight and had high blood pressure and cholesterol. She never had a lot of energy to really do much (this I remember so well). She was sedentary and tired most of the time and would quickly lose her breath with exertion.

But then something changed. I remember her telling me that her doctor spoke to her about the benefits of eating healthy, specifically with more fruits and vegetables, and exercising. She spent time reading about these topics and would tell me about the things she learned. I would visit her on weekends and we would prepare the family meals together. While we were cooking together, she would tell me about the benefits of various ingredients we were using and why they were healthy for me.

This was when I first heard about the benefits of avocados, tomatoes, and bananas. (Some of the healthy Mediterranean recipes she passed down to me are included in the appendix, page 183.) Along with eating healthy, my grandparents turned their den into an exercise room with a stationary bike, rowing machine, and treadmill. Then her body transformed. She lost a lot of weight, and I know from talking to her as I got older that she decreased her blood pressure and cholesterol medications. She felt better, had more energy, and was more mobile. She wanted to do things. She was happy. She also exuded radiance and beauty as she began to enjoy life again. This made a huge impression on me and is something that I think about with my own children.

Healthy eating and exercise and treating our bodies right make such a huge difference and for some people, may even allow them to decrease or go off medications like my grandmother did. The wrong foods trigger inflammation throughout the body, and the right foods nourish us, quelling this inflammation. (Harvard School of Public Health, 2014)

Numerous studies have pointed to this systemic or body-wide inflammation as one of the leading triggers for premature aging in the body and on the skin and it is a leading cause of chronic diseases. (Maraki et al, 2015) But we know that a healthy, whole foods diet like the Mediterranean diet reduces inflammation, as shown in one study conducted by Italian researchers and published in the *Journal of the American College of Cardiology*.

Combine These Foods for Better Health

There's increasing proof that what you eat is as important as what you combine it with. Some healthy food combinations include:

Tomatoes and broccoli

Eating tomatoes and broccoli together was shown, in one University of Illinois study, to be better at fighting cancer than each individual food was alone.

Tomatoes and avocados

Fats make carotenoids more bioavailable, which means that the body is better able to use them. And adding olive oil (another healthy fat) to pasta sauce, a Mediterranean staple, makes the antioxidants in the pasta sauce more available to the body, says one study in the *Asia Pacific Journal of Clinical Nutrition*.

Berries and grapes

Eating a variety of antioxidant-rich fruits gives you a more powerful antioxidant punch, say researchers at Cornell University's Department of Food Science. The idea is that you don't have to limit yourself to one or two: make a fruit salad and you'll get even more health-protective benefits.

Green tea, dark chocolate, and apples

This makes a healthy afternoon snack because research from the National University of Singapore shows that the catechins (powerful polyphenols, or antioxidants) in green tea and chocolate work synergistically with quercetin (a flavonoid or another powerful antioxidant) found in apples and onions. Together, they work to loosen clumpy blood platelets, improving cardiovascular health.

Curry and black pepper

Research from St. John's Medical College in India shows that turmeric (a key component of curry), which has powerful anti-inflammatory benefits, is better absorbed when combined with black pepper.

Chronic Inflammation and Your Health

Inflammation is actually the core of our body's healing and immune response. When something harmful or irritating affects a part of our body, an inflammatory cascade of events is set into motion: blood flow increases to that area, and along with it, healing proteins and infection-fighting white blood cells. Without inflammation, wounds and infections would never heal. (Giugliano et al, 2006)

As with stress, though, some inflammation is healthy, but chronic inflammation is not. An unhealthy diet is one of the key triggers of inflammation. A Mediterranean diet, however, can nourish your body and skin with the right nutrients, and prevent and even reduce chronic inflammation, contributing to more youthful body and more radiant, glowing, and healthy (a.k.a. more youthful-looking) skin. (Galland, 2010)

Inflammation has also been called "skin enemy number one" for good reason. It's been linked to skin problems like acne, rosacea, eczema, and psoriasis. In fact, researchers at Northwestern University found that people with inflammatory conditions like eczema have been found to have an increased risk of heart disease and stroke, a possible long-term effect of chronic inflammation within the body. (Wadyka, 2011; Silverberg et al, 2015; Bowe et al, 2012)

How to Eat for a Healthier You

The core principals of eating, below, incorporate the Mediterranean style of eating that helps to reduce inflammation in the body and keep you healthy.

Eat locally grown fruits and vegetables whenever possible.

Locally grown produce is more nutritious and just plain better for you. Many nutrients, particularly heat- and light-sensitive vitamins B and C, are lost in the shipping process, as are fat-soluble nutrients like vitamins A and E and carotenoids (including lycopene), so if you can buy produce from your local farm or farmer's market that doesn't have to be shipped, you'll be getting more nutrients. (Barrett, 2019)

The nutrient content of spinach, particularly its folate (vitamin B_9) and carotenoid content, gets quickly lost the longer it's stored. The faster fresh food makes it to your table (the idea behind the popular food-to-table movement), the more nutritious that food will be for you. There is one exception: frozen fruits and vegetables. These foods are picked at the height of their freshness and undergo a process called flash freezing (often done right where they're picked) allowing them to avoid the loss of nutrients from shipping and storage. (Pandrangi et al, 2004)

Another way to be sure you're getting enough key nutrients: eat the peels. The color of a fruit or vegetable is concentrated in the peel, and it's this colorful part that can be a concentrated source of antioxidants called phytochemicals. Tomatoes, for example, have 98 percent of their flavonols (powerful phytochemicals or antioxidants) in their skins. And, in the case of potatoes, the skin has more antioxidants, iron, potassium, B vitamins, and fiber than the flesh. The peels are also good sources of something called insoluble fiber, which helps keep you regular. Some peels (like that of an apple) are also rich in soluble fiber that's been shown to help lower cholesterol and control blood sugar. (Bonwick et al, 2013; Newswise, 2014; University of California Berkeley, 2019)

What's more, how you cook your fruits and vegetables, fresh or frozen, matters too. Overcooking vegetables like broccoli can deplete heat-sensitive nutrients like vitamins C and B. If you do have to cook them, lightly steam them to maintain their antioxidant levels. (Frying causes a significantly higher loss of antioxidants.) My rule of thumb for steaming is once you can visibly see the steam, turn off the heat and let the steam cook the vegetables for a few more minutes. Then check to make sure the vegetables are still bright green (in the case of broccoli) and still slightly crisp. Once they're done, remove the lid and let the steam out. (Miglio et al, 2008, Barbour, 2009, Dewanto et al, 2002)

Eat less red meat.

Red meat should be limited, if possible, to less than four times a month. Research published in the *American Journal of Clinical Nutrition* has found that the more red meat you eat, the higher your markers of inflammation. Eating red meat has also been linked to chronic diseases like breast cancer. (Cho et al, 2010; Harvard School of Public Health, 2019)

If you're going to eat red meat once in a while, look for grass-fed red meat, which is rich in inflammation-quelling omega-3 fatty acids. And bake, poach, stew, or steam it, but don't char it. Doing so has been shown to increase the formation of carcinogenic compounds called AGEs, or advanced glycation end products. The more char, the more AGEs. (van Heijst et al, 2005; Medical News Today, 2014; The Guardian, 2014)

Using rosemary, an herb high in health-promoting antioxidants, on your meat before grilling it can also help reduce the formation of unhealthy AGEs. Soaking meat in a vinegar- or citrus-based marinade, along with antioxidant-rich herbs like rosemary, also helps reduce AGEs. (ScienceDaily, 2007)

Incorporate olive oil into your daily diet.

Extra virgin olive oil is a staple of the Mediterranean style of eating. Not only is olive oil delicious, but it's healthy for you too, because it contains very high levels of monounsaturated fats that may be linked to a reduced risk of heart disease. Because extra virgin olive oil is the first extract from the olives, it's typically cold pressed and not heat processed. This allows for a higher concentration of antioxidants. (Keys et al, 1986; Owen et al, 2000)

Olive oil can help repair skin damage, soothe and relieve chapped, itchy skin, and help rebuild skin's moisture barrier, which keeps skin hydrated. It's no surprise, then, that researchers found—as published in the journal *Burns*—that when burn patients consumed olive oil, their wounds healed faster than patients who didn't consume olive oil. The reason, researchers theorized, is that olive oil has significant anti-inflammatory and antioxidant benefits, which help to optimize wound healing. (Najmi et al, 2014; Covas, 2007)

Just to show you how powerful a health food olive oil is: adding as little as ten teaspoons of olive oil to your daily diet could help protect against breast cancer. What's more, compelling research from scientists at Rutgers University in New Jersey found that oleocanthal, a powerful antioxidant found in extra virgin olive oil, has been shown to wipe out cancer cells in as little as thirty minutes. This is the kind of science that's so impressive it's hard not to sit up and take notice or at least revamp your diet to be more like the Ikarians. (Branson, 2015)

Look for olive oils that come in a dark bottle, which protects against light. Exposure to light can cause the oil to deteriorate. Also, steer clear of giant tins. Olive oils are best used within three to six months. To keep it fresh, store your oil in a cool, dark place.

Get enough probiotics.

These healthy bacteria, found in everything from yogurt and kefir to fermented foods, have been found to keep you healthy. In fact, our bodies are pretty active petri dishes. There's a mix of good and bad bacteria living inside each of us, from our skin (where a few hundred species have been identified) to our intestines. It's been estimated that the human body is composed of 10 percent human cells and 90 percent bacteria. This means human cells are outnumbered by bacteria thirty-three to one! This mix of bacteria inside us is often referred to as the human microbiome. (Barros, 2015)

Nowhere is this microbiome more evident than in the gut. Bacteria line the intestines and help you digest food. During this process of digestion, they make essential vitamins, send signals to the immune system, and create small molecules that can help your brain function properly.

Adding different kinds of healthy bacteria into our bodies, through diet or supplements, can help reduce gas and bloating and increase regularity. These bacteria in the gut are also responsible for the production of the feel-good chemical serotonin, according to researchers at the California Institute of Technology. (It's estimated that 90 percent of the body's serotonin is made in the digestive tract.) What this means: a healthy digestive system, with the right balance of bacteria, can make a huge difference in relaxation levels and mood, a key role of serotonin in the body.

A healthy gut is also critical to a healthy immune system. In fact, 70 to 80 percent of our immune tissue is located in the digestive system. It also seems that a healthy gut regulates levels of the body's main antioxidant, glutathione, which fights a host of diseases. (Mardinoglu et al, 2015; Quigley, 2013)

What's more, healthy bacteria in the gut has also been shown to help with acne relief. An overgrowth of bad bacteria in the body, however, can trigger inflammation in the body and skin problems like acne, psoriasis, and dermatitis, say researchers from Case Western Reserve University. Healthy bacteria also seem to help increase the production of ceramides or lipid molecules found on the surface layer of the skin, helping to restore the skin's barrier function. It's this barrier function that's critical to keeping out chemicals, bacteria, and sunlight and keeping in the good stuff like moisture. The right balance of bacteria *on* the skin contributes to the defense mechanisms of the skin and proper immune system functioning. That's why an imbalance on the skin, as in the gut, can contribute to conditions like atopic dermatitis. (ScienceDaily, 2015; McNamee, 2014; Healy, 2014; Goodrich et al, 2019; Rupani, 2015; Salem et al, 2018; Johnson, 2014)

Opt for glass, porcelain, or stainless-steel containers.

Store food in glass containers and avoid eating or drinking from plastic containers. Plastics contain chemicals that have been linked to health problems like cancer.

One study found that men, women, and children exposed to high levels of phthalates (chemicals found in plastics, including in some plastic baby teethers and some personal care products) tend to have reduced levels of testosterone in their blood compared to those with lower chemical exposure. While testosterone is the main sex hormone in men, it contributes to a variety of functions in both men and women, including physical growth and strength, brain function, bone density, and cardiovascular health. (Jobling et al, 1995; Meeker et al, 2014)

Extensive exposure to common chemicals found in plastics has also been linked to an earlier start of menopause in women. What's more, according to a study published in the journal *Human Reproduction*, even low levels of exposure to phthalates by mothers who were pregnant affected male infants' reproductive health later in life. Here are some helpful tips on how to limit your exposure. (Grindler et al, 2015; Swan et al, 2015)

Avoid microwaving polycarbonate plastic food containers.

It seems that glass-like plastics like polycarbonate are solid, but they're not. They're made from synthetic, non-natural materials that seem durable but often cannot withstand heat, meaning they break down from overuse at high temperatures. A break down in plastics causes chemicals in the plastics to potentially leach into food or drink.

A good rule of thumb to follow is to avoid microwaving any kind of plastic, including plastic containers and plastic wrap. I would also argue, for this same reason, to use caution when putting plastic dishes in the dishwasher. The top rack is often cooler than the bottom rack and may not heat up the plastic as much. Or hand wash them in warm, not hot, water instead.

Know that BPA-free doesn't mean chemical-free.

BPA is an industrial chemical used primarily to make hard poly-carbonate plastic and other types of plastics. This is actually the chemical that hardens plastics. It's found in many products including some dental sealants, water bottles, and in the lining of many canned foods and drinks. The problem with this chemical is that it's an endocrine disruptor; endocrine is a chemical that mimics hormones in the body like estrogen. This hormone mimicking triggers oxidative damage and long-term health problems like cancer and has been linked to higher blood pressure, according to one study published in the journal *Hypertension*. And just because something has been labeled BPA-free doesn't mean that it doesn't contain other potentially harmful chemicals. Many of the replacements for BPA, though labeled "safe," have not been thoroughly tested for their effects on your health. (National Institutes of Health; 2019; Bhan et al, 2014; Bae et al, 2014; Rochester et al, 2015)

Reduce your use of canned foods.

My philosophy when it comes to food: fresh is always best. When you can't use fresh, frozen is the next best option. Canned food is typically high in sodium and low in nutrients, which is why I try to avoid it. If you do want to use canned, be sure to check the labels to find ones that contain low to no sodium. The average American takes in anywhere from 3,000 to 3,600 mg of sodium daily, but the body only needs about 200 mg per day. That's a big discrepancy. Too much sodium causes high blood pressure and can make your eyes and face look puffy. By choosing whole, fresh foods over canned, processed foods, you can drastically cut down your daily sodium intake. (American Heart Association, 2019)

The Mediterranean diet is naturally low in sodium, as is the DASH diet. This DASH diet borrows many of the healthy eating principles of the Mediterranean diet (eating fresh fruits and vegetables, unrefined grains, nuts/seeds, legumes, lean protein, and healthy fats) but also focuses on reducing sodium overall by limiting the amount of processed foods you're eating and the amount of table salt you add to foods.

A National Institutes of Health study showed that by following the DASH diet, you may be able to reduce your blood pressure by a few points in just two weeks and your systolic blood pressure (which results from your heart muscle contracting) could drop by seven to twelve points over time. This could make a significant difference in your long-term health. (ScienceDaily, 2001)

Eat seasonally.
Eating foods when nature produces them is something the Mediterranean culture and people all over the world have done throughout history. At its very core, seasonal eating is local eating. It means building your meals around foods that have been harvested at their peak on local farms and it means modifying your diet according to the season.

When the food you're eating isn't in season (i.e., you're eating watermelon in winter), it's either been grown in a greenhouse or shipped in from other parts of the world, both of which affect taste and nutrient content. When transporting crops, they must be harvested early and refrigerated so they don't rot during transportation. They may not ripen as effectively as they would in their natural environment and, as a result, they don't develop their full flavor. In addition, transporting produce sometimes requires irradiation (zapping the produce with a burst of radiation to kill germs) and preservatives (such as petroleum-based wax) to protect the produce and increase shelf life.

Many cultures, including Indian culture and its ancient medicine ayurveda, believe that nature harvests the antidotes for the season. For example, warming and nourishing foods like root vegetables, soups and stews, and fermented foods like tempeh and kimchi help to build protein and fat reserves in the body for the long winter season ahead. According to ayurveda, our digestive fires have evolved to be stronger in winter, allowing us to eat more dense foods than we would in summer. In summer, our fires are weaker, which allows us to eat less-dense foods like salads and fresh berries. (Douillard, 2001)

Eat fish.
Everything from wild-caught salmon and sardines to tilapia contain healthy fats called essential fatty acids. (They're also found in non-fish foods like flaxseeds, chia seeds, and walnuts.) Studies have shown that these fats can do everything from boosting your mood to protecting cognitive function and preventing Alzheimer's disease and cancer. One reason they have such a health-promoting effect is that they decrease inflammation. (Parker et al, 2006)

Add more color to your diet.
The more colorful the food, the higher the content of health-promoting antioxidants. Some of my favorite colorful, antioxidant-rich foods include berries (acai berries, blueberries, raspberries, strawberries, and blackberries), citrus fruits like red grapefruit and oranges, leafy greens, pomegranates, and grapes. (Whitehead et al, 2012; Wang et al, 2008)

Here's a guide to what colorful fruits and vegetables can offer you and your health:

> **Green:** Veggies like kale, spinach, purslane (similar to watercress and spinach), and broccoli are high in lutein, which helps keep your vision sharp. They're also high in the antioxidant vitamin C, which is critical for healthy, youthful looking skin and the production of collagen, the tissue-firming protein that acts as a scaffold for the skin.

> **Yellow/Orange:** Mangoes, carrots, sweet potatoes, and pumpkin all contain antioxidants called carotenoids that can reduce the risk of developing cancer, report researchers from Tufts University in Boston. They can also give your complexion the healthy glow so often used to characterize youthful skin.

> **Blue/Purple:** Berries like blueberries, acai berries, and blackberries, as well as purple potatoes and purple cauliflower, are chock-full of antioxidant-rich substances called anthocyanins. A study from Ohio State University College of Medicine found that anthocyanins prevent tumors from forming, including tumors on the skin, and may even suppress their growth.

> **Red:** Watermelon and tomatoes are rich in lycopene (a carotenoid), which may protect against cancer and heart disease and boosts your skin's radiance. Lycopene also has a natural, UV-protective capability. This doesn't mean, though, that you don't need sunscreen. You do. This natural sun protection is just another reason eating healthy, including colorful fruits and vegetables, can slow down the aging process of the skin, particularly when it's exposed to the damaging effects of the

sun's ultraviolet rays. (Ho et al, 2014; Arab et al, 2000; Raloff, 2001))

Enjoy dark chocolate in moderation.

White sugar may increase inflammation and reduce immunity, but that doesn't mean you need to forgo sweets altogether. Dark chocolate, with at least 70 percent cocoa content, is one of the healthiest sweets you can indulge in, in moderation. It's chock-full of substances called flavonoids, which are part of a group of antioxidants known as polyphenols (the same antioxidants found in green tea and grapes). Dark chocolate also contains minerals like calcium, magnesium, and potassium, which are good for the body and for the skin.

In one study, German scientists found that eating dark chocolate, specifically half a cup of dark chocolate cocoa daily, resulted, after just one month, in skin that was smoother, more hydrated, and less scaly and red when exposed to ultraviolet light. These scientists speculated that the flavonoids help absorb UV light, protecting the skin and increasing blood flow, as well as hydration. (Esser et al, 2013; Heinrich et al, 2006)

Cook with fresh herbs.

All herbs, like sage, thyme, peppermint, and lemon balm, are rich in antioxidants that can help fight inflammation. Many herbs, like oregano, are also antimicrobial. In fact, oregano contains an active agent called rosmarinic acid that's super high in free-radical-fighting antioxidants. Use them when you're cooking or just sprinkle them on anything you can, to add flavor and antioxidants.

Cut down on the amount of sugar you eat.

Anything that causes a fast spike in blood sugar levels, like white sugar and white flour (found in many processed foods), triggers an inflammatory response in the body. Eat it on a regular basis and you're keeping your inflammation levels on overdrive.

Sugar has also been known to impair immune function: One landmark study, published in the *American Journal of Clinical Nutrition*, found that consuming 100 grams (just 3.5 ounces) of carbohydrates, such as fructose, glucose, sucrose, and honey, inhibited the ability of white blood cells to destroy harmful microorganisms in the body by as much as 50 percent. This impairment of immune function began less than thirty minutes after sugar ingestion and remained this way for more than five hours. (Sanchez et al, 1973)

But don't use chemical sweeteners as a sugar substitute. Chemical sweeteners seem to fool the body so the body doesn't register that it's consumed sugar, causing us to eat more than we should. In fact, a study from the University of Texas Health Science Center indicates that artificial sweeteners, found in diet sodas, could cause weight gain by stimulating the development of new fat cells. (Fowler et al, 2015)

Drink enough water.

I can't emphasize enough the importance of drinking plain old water. Water helps the body rid itself of toxins. If you drink enough, it flushes out the kidneys and pulls toxins from the body. If you don't drink enough water, your body can't filter properly. And if you get dehydrated, the organs don't function as well. When it comes to the skin, proper hydration makes the skin smoother and "plumper" looking, more hydrated, and more radiant overall. Dehydration can cause fine lines and wrinkles to become more obvious.

If you dislike the taste of plain water, mix in your own healthy flavoring by adding antioxidant-rich frozen organic berries, cold organic cucumbers, or even a splash of fruit juice.

Replace saturated fats.

These are found in everything from fatty meats (beef, lamb, pork) to butter, cheese, and dairy products made from whole or two percent milk, and can be replaced with monounsaturated or polyunsaturated fats (found in olives, olive oil, avocados, flaxseed, walnuts, and fish oil).

It's a good idea to also try to eliminate trans fats from your diet by avoiding fast food like french fries and processed foods like cookies and pastries. Trans fats are also found in solid shortening and stick margarine. One study in the *Journal of the National Cancer Institute* found that women who had the highest levels of trans fats in their blood were twice as likely as women with the lowest blood levels to develop breast cancer. (Cho et al, 2019)

Be sure you're getting enough vitamin D.

This essential nutrient (actually a hormone) is getting a lot of attention these days for good reason. Not only does it play an important role, alongside calcium, in strengthening bones, it's also a powerful antioxidant and potent immune booster.

Vitamin D is known as the sun vitamin because the body produces it when exposed to the sun. (Our bodies aren't able to produce vitamin D on their own.) But there are plenty of ways to get your daily D without sun exposure, which puts you at risk of skin cancer and premature skin aging. Eat foods rich in vitamin D like salmon, sardines, and dairy, or check in with your doctor about whether you should take a daily supplement. Adults need anywhere from 400 IU to 800 IU daily. Also important: Look for vitamin D_3 (or cholecalciferol) instead of vitamin D_2 (called ergocalciferol) on your supplements. Vitamin D_3 is the most readily absorbed and utilized by the body.

Try spicy foods.

Red chili peppers (also called cayenne peppers) contain an ingredient called capsaicin, which makes the peppers incredibly hot to the taste. This fire and heat in the mouth actually triggers the brain to produce a rush of endorphins, the feel-good chemicals that block pain, from arthritis pain to the pain of itchy, inflamed skin. Capsaicin has also been shown by researchers in South Korea to inhibit inflammation in the body. (Kim et al, 2003)

What's more, this hot spice has also been shown by researchers at the Chinese University of Hong Kong to lower blood pressure, reduce cholesterol levels, and reduce risk of blood clots, boosting cardiovascular health. It's no surprise then that additional researchers have now determined that eating spicy foods (including foods that contain red hot chili peppers) can boost longevity. Harvard Medical School researchers have found that capsaicin has antioxidant, anti-obesity, anti-inflammation, and anti-cancer properties. (American Chemical Society, 2012; Ly et al, 2015)

A word of warning, though: as health-promoting as spicy foods can be, they can still aggravate skin conditions like rosacea, which flare up in response to heat and spices. If you struggle with rosacea, use caution with spicy foods and capsaicin.

Enjoy a cup of coffee.

One staple of a Mediterranean diet: a cup (or two) of coffee every day. I've always loved a cup of coffee in the morning, but I've come to love it even more over the years as new research from the Harvard School of Public Health backs up coffee's health benefits, namely that it does everything from keep your heart healthy and lower your cancer risk to lowering depression and helping you live longer. This is thanks to the fact that coffee is full of health-promoting antioxidants. Moderation is key, however. (MPR, 2015; Goodman, 2014; Rosendahl et al, 2015; Loftfield et al, 2015; Conley, 2012; Ramanujan, 2014; Lucas et al, 2011; Rivas, 2014; Eskelinen, 2010)

If you like coffee, try these new ways to spice up your cup and add extra health benefits.

> **Cardamom:** Grind a few cardamom seeds into grounds and you'll be adding antioxidant minerals like manganese, magnesium, and zinc.

> **Cayenne:** Love spicy foods? Then you'll want to add a dash of this to coffee grounds to give your morning joe a kick. When you do, you'll be enhancing it with antioxidant flavonoids, as well as a small dose of vitamin C, B6, potassium, and manganese.

> **Cinnamon:** Add a dash or two to your coffee grounds and you'll be mixing in the mineral manganese.

> **Cocoa powder:** Mix unsweetened cocoa powder into coffee grounds to add antioxidant flavonoids, as well as fiber, iron, and magnesium.

Keep in mind that if you don't like coffee or can't drink coffee for health reasons, you're not losing out. There are plenty of other ways to get your daily dose of antioxidants, namely fruits and vegetables and tea.

Have some tea.

Coffee isn't the only drink with benefits. There are different types of tea, all with varying health advantages. Here's a guide:

- **Green tea** is made from non-wilted leaves that aren't oxidized and it contains high concentrations of flavonoids. (It contains little caffeine.) Numerous researchers from around the world have proven the anti-inflammatory benefits of green tea. The reason? Green tea contains an extremely high concentration of powerful antioxidants called catechins.

- **Black tea** is produced when tea leaves are wilted, bruised, rolled, and fully oxidized. (Shortly after harvesting, tea leaves begin to wilt and oxidize. During oxidation, chemicals in the leaves are broken down by enzymes, resulting in darkening of the leaves.) It has fewer antioxidants than green tea. The more processed a tea is, the less flavonoids it contains. And it contains more caffeine than green tea.

- **Herbal teas** are naturally caffeine-free and can give you a dose of herbs along with a comforting drink that you can have any time of the day. These teas are made from the fruits, seeds, or roots of plants. They have lower concentrations of antioxidants than green, black, oolong, and white teas, but they are a good option for anyone avoiding caffeine.

- **Oolong tea** is made from wilted, bruised, and partially oxidized leaves, creating an intermediate kind of tea that's midway between green and black teas. It contains moderate amounts of antioxidants and caffeine. It has the body of black tea with the freshness of green tea.

- **White tea** is made from young leaves or growth buds that have undergone minimal oxidation, meaning it's the least processed of all teas. Because of this, white tea is able to retain its extremely high concentration of antioxidants. It also contains the least caffeine of all teas. It has the most delicate flavor and aroma. (Mukherjee et al, 2014; Tipoe et al, 2007; Cavet et al, 2011)

Eat nuts and seeds.

Nuts and seeds (think pumpkin seeds, sunflower seeds, chia seeds, and flaxseeds) are probably some of the healthiest snacks around, which is why they're integral to a Mediterranean diet. Munching on nuts and seeds or nut/seed butter really does the body and the skin good. One reason: nuts and seeds like almonds and walnuts are high in healthy monounsaturated fats, the same type of health-promoting fats found in olive oil. They're also high in protein, antioxidants, and key nutrients like fiber, protein, magnesium, potassium, and vitamin E. (Arab et al, 2015)

Nuts also contain selenium, a nutrient important for many biological functions like immune response, fertility, and thyroid hormone production. Selenium is also a powerful antioxidant.

Where Do You Go from Here?

Put these healthy diet strategies into practice and I guarantee that you'll be on your way to a healthy body and healthy skin for years to come. Don't get discouraged, though, if you can't follow all of these diet tips at once. The best way to institute healthy eating is to incorporate one or two (or even three) strategies into your life for twenty-one days, the amount of time it takes for a habit to become ingrained. Then you can incorporate more strategies as you're ready to take another step on your journey toward health and longevity and inner and outer beauty.

Remember: health is not a race. Slow and steady good habits, particularly when it comes to your diet, is what wins in the end. In the words of Virginia Woolf, "One cannot think well, love well, sleep well, if one has not dined well."

CHAPTER 4

EXERCISE AS SPIRITUAL MOVEMENT

VISUALIZE YOURSELF WALKING DOWN a tree-lined pathway, the sun's rays beaming down through the trees, a gentle breeze on your face, listening to the sound of your breath in and out. There's something very meditative about moving your body, particularly in the outdoors. Movement is so much more than just burning calories and building muscles, though these are important benefits for your health. In modern society, we focus so much on getting to the gym to fit in our workout, with our headphones on, that we forget about connecting with the world around us during the process. Maybe this is a reason why so many of us find it hard to stick to an exercise regimen, particularly one that seems like a chore rather than a celebration of our bodies, which is what exercise should be.

Movement not only works your muscles, including your heart muscle, it also clears the brain, focuses you, and makes you feel great, thanks to the hormones called endorphins that are released during exercise. Endorphins are often referred to as feel-good hormones because they do just that: they boost your mood, making you feel happy and energized. (These are what give you the so-called euphoric runner's high.)

These endorphins are one of the reasons exercise lowers stress, helping you look at the world around you differently and with greater optimism, enthusiasm, and happiness. This reduction in stress helps you fall asleep quickly and sleep more soundly, according to the National Sleep Foundation. Regular movement also boosts your immunity, reducing how often you get sick. And it gives your skin a youthful glow. There's a reason healthy radiance is common after a heart-pumping workout: as you breathe in oxygen and work your muscles, you boost your circulation, increasing blood flow to the skin. As circulation and sweat increases, so does the removal of toxins from the body, which in turn contributes to your overall health. (Sforzo, 1989)

I want to share the story of one of my patients, Jessica, who came to see me because of chronic eczema that wouldn't stop flaring up. Like so many working mothers today, Jessica hadn't really worked out for years after having her third child. Sure, she fit in an exercise class here or there, but she didn't really move with any consistency. Jessica also wasn't eating well. I prescribed her a skin cream to help with the eczema, but we also discussed how lifestyle, including exercise, plays a part in inflammatory skin conditions like eczema. I explained to her that taking care of their body is one of the most important gifts a parent can give their children. Having your children see that you are important, that you are prioritizing yourself, and that you are moving provides a lot of healthy life lessons for them to learn. Committing to movement is an affirmation that you are grateful for your body and are doing everything you can to celebrate that.

Another thing Jessica and I spoke about was that exercise does not have to be a chore. If it feels that way, then you're definitely doing the wrong kind of exercise. When it feels right, you love it and want to do more of it. She explained that she hated the exercise boot camp class she forced herself to do every once in a while. She loved walking, however. But Jessica always believed that walking wasn't effective exercise because she wasn't burning enough calories to "count." Nothing could be further from the truth. Walking is one of the most effective body-mind-spirit exercises you can do, particularly if you do it regularly. Jessica committed to finding time to walk every day. Like all my patients who make over their lifestyles after meeting with me, when Jessica came back for a follow-up one month later, she was feeling better about herself and exuded more confidence. Her eczema was dramatically reduced and her lifestyle had gotten a makeover. She was walking outdoors every single day, except for when it was pouring rain. At first, she started with a quick mind-clearing walk around the block. Then she built up to walking around her local park several times a week. As she explained it to me, "I love walking and always have. I dropped several pounds, am sleeping better, and am less stressed around my kids. I have a whole new appreciation for life!" The key, as with Jessica, is to do something you love. Walking, dancing, yoga, swimming, and tai chi are all movement options that can be meditative and spiritual, while also being good for the body.

The Mind-Exercise Connection

The brain functions better after exercise. This connection has been proven again and again by researchers. I also discovered this connection firsthand during medical school. I had a treadmill in my apartment, and despite long, grueling study hours and practical training in the hospital, I made it a point to walk on the treadmill four or five times a week. I tried to do anywhere between thirty minutes and an hour. A few light weights for strength training, regular stretching, and exercise videos helped complete my not-so-fancy apartment routine. This commitment to exercise—in spite of my busy schedule—made all the difference for me. It cleared my mind so I could process everything better. I also felt better in general—I was less stressed and happier overall. Plus, I had more energy. And I got sick much less than I ever did before, despite having a demanding workload.

I previously mentioned the endorphins that give you the runner's high. These hormones are actually what are called neurotransmitters, chemicals that pass electrical signals from one neuron to the next in the nervous system. These neurotransmitters play a key role in the functioning of the central nervous system. When they're released, as they are after exercise, they interact with what are called opiate receptors in the brain, reducing our perception of pain. That's why endorphins have a similar, albeit natural and non-addictive, effect on the brain like the powerful drugs morphine and codeine, which act on these same receptors.

These endorphins, which are released during moderate to vigorous exercise, are certainly one reason why exercise can reduce anxiety. But *all* forms of exercise, from gentle yoga and tai chi to swimming, walking, and dance, reduce stress, so there's more to the mind-body picture than just endorphins. I believe it has to do with the meditative and spiritual aspect of moving our bodies. By being aware of our bodies during exercise and by being appreciative of all that our bodies can do, we are experiencing a critical mind-body connection that helps relax us and connect us with our spiritual selves. This is even more the case if your mind is able to wander away from the day's worries and focus on the here and now—your rhythmic breathing, the sound of your feet hitting the pavement while you're running, the feel of the wind on your face. You can even recite a mantra like this one to yourself while exercising: "I lovingly do everything I can to assist my body in maintaining perfect health."

One young teenage patient of mine, Madison, shared the reason she loves swimming, particularly what's considered long-course laps. She loved feeling the water on her body and being able to tune out the world around her and just swim. She also used her swimming time to think about things, working out issues in her mind. Madison's mother explained to me that Madison is always much calmer getting out of the pool than she was getting in. Her mom also mentioned to me how much more self-confident Madison was after having started swimming. These benefits of exercise are not part of the popular calorie-counting and fat-burning reasons to get moving, but I would argue they are just as important for your health.

Vigorous exercise like power walking, running, swimming, and biking can also boost brain functioning, helping you think more clearly and stay alert and focused longer, while allowing you to be more creative. In fact, research from the University of British Columbia shows that moving the body is actually so powerful it causes the creation of new neurons or nerve cells in the brain, and specifically the hippocampus, the center of learning and memory. Stress, on the other hand, hampers the growth of new neurons. What's more, a study from the University of California San Diego School of Medicine found that exercise also seems to boost the brain by reducing inflammation in the body and in the brain, keeping brain cells healthy. The researchers even go so far as to say that exercise actually changes the brain for the better, protecting it from age-related memory changes. In essence, exercise keeps the brain young. (ten Brinke et al, 2014; Barry, 2011; Dinitrov, 2017; Sandoiu, 2017)

Keep in mind too that the head is home to the crown and third eye chakras. By boosting brainpower and circulation all over the body, including in the head, meditative exercise helps to open the crown and third eye chakras, particularly when you're breathing in and out rhythmically, as is the case during vigorous exercise. Remember, it is the crown chakra that rules our communication with our spiritual self, while our third eye chakra governs intuition, memory, and imagination.

Movement Meditation

To transform current ideals of exercise away from the treadmill, elliptical trainer, and exercise classes, we must look to movement as meditation. We must consider movement as an opportunity to sync the body and spirit. Doing so can re-energize us, make us more creative, and lift anxiety and depression.

What this means: we need to approach exercise with a different mindset. Get outdoors instead of going to the gym. Take off your headphones and listen to the sounds around you. Observe what's going on while staying centered and focused on a sound or mantra. Try this while doing any outdoor activity: walking your dog; running in the park; biking around your neighborhood; or kayaking, canoeing, or stand-up paddle boarding. You don't have to go fast. You just have to be mindful of everything around you—how the sun shines or the clouds roll in, the feel of the air on your skin, the sounds of nature or others around you. Try to observe, hear, smell, and feel without attachment.

I mentioned forest bathing earlier (see page 70), but this is the perfect example of movement meditation. Forest bathing, also called *shinrin* ("forest") *yoku* ("bathing"), is the act of taking in the forest through all your senses: the smell of the earth beneath your feet, the feel of the fresh, cold water of the stream, the sounds of the birds around you, the taste of the dew in the air, and visions of the beauty in every direction. (ShinrinYoku, 2019)

The idea behind forest bathing is that nature can restore and rejuvenate us. The key: you must turn off your phone and pack it away while forest bathing. This means no pictures for Instagram or texts of what you're seeing along the way. To effectively forest bathe, you must disconnect from the rest of the world around you. When doing this with others, it's most effective to limit conversation. All of this allows you to connect with nature, which brings a sense of calm. The beauty of forest bathing, however, is that you don't need a forest and you don't need to walk. You can perform the actions of forest bathing while doing any activity, as long as it's done outdoors in nature.

Healing Water Movement

For thousands of years, people have sought relief and renewal—physical, emotional, and even spiritual—by immersing themselves in water. We come from water in the womb, which is why it has the power to relax our bodies and soothe our souls. Water is also associated with the sacral chakra, located in the pelvic area. When this chakra is open, you are calm, joyful, creative, and connect easily with others. These are also the benefits of water-based movement.

There's no question about the healing powers of water, which is why water-based movement like swimming, with its blissful weightlessness, can be done by most people at any age. It's also incredibly peaceful and meditative if you're in the pool without a lot of noise or other swimmers. My teenage patient Madison found this out firsthand.

Swimming is actually excellent exercise for the body too, something that most people don't realize. I absolutely love to swim. It utilizes arms, legs, and core, which keeps all of them toned. And whether you're doing laps, aqua aerobics, aqua jogging (running in the water), or even aqua kickboxing, you're getting your heart rate up, without the impact on joints or muscles that land-based exercises like running or jumping can have. (Water acts as a cushion for the body's joints; it's low impact.) The water also provides up to 42 percent greater resistance than air, making it the perfect weight-training machine.

There are plenty of water-based movements that also involve meditation. Consider meditative stand-up paddle boarding and kayaking or canoeing. And there's the water-based movement called Watsu, which comes from a combination of the words "water" and "shiatsu." During a Watsu session, which occurs in a warm pool heated to the same temperature as your body, the Watsu practitioner supports, cradles, and gently rocks you in a way not so different from what happens in a womb. The practitioner takes you through a series of gentle stretches meant to calm the body and mind. The warm water relaxes the muscles, helping you get a deep, relaxing stretch. You can also do it on your own in a warm "therapy" pool, with this meditation. (Watsu, 2019)

Warm Water Meditation

Close your eyes and feel the water around you, touching your skin, moving with a gentle rhythm like your own breath. Imagine yourself as one with the water. Appreciate the comfort and safety of the water around you. Feel the cooler air on your face and neck.

Visualize yourself swimming in the ocean. Feel the rhythmic waves syncing with the rhythms in your own body. Feel the heat of the sun on your face. Smell the salt from the ocean air.

Take a deep diaphragmatic breath in and exhale deeply. Now, try Ujjayi (pronounced *ooo-ji*), or ocean breath, which helps to further calm the body and mind through its rhythm, which is said to mimic the rhythm of the ocean waves. Close your lips and breathe deeply in through your nose. Now open your mouth and breathe out saying "haaah" as if you were trying to fog up a mirror. Continue this ocean breath five times: breathe in deeply, and breathe out "haaah." Finish by taking a long, slow, deep breath in and out through your mouth.

Yoga: Exercise for the Body and Spirit

Yoga, as I talked about earlier, helps you breathe, relax, and stretch at the same time. It also exercises the body without putting strain on the muscles, making it appropriate for people of any age, even for those with illnesses, disabilities, and disease when other forms of exercise may not be an option. Yoga combines both meditation and motion, making it a good exercise option for busy, stressed people, which includes so many of us today. One of the great things about yoga is that you don't need to go anywhere to do it. It can be done in your living room or even in your office, no gym necessary.

But one question so often comes up: can yoga *really* provide the health and cardiovascular benefits of exercise like an intense cardio workout can? The answer is yes, but it depends on what kind of yoga you're practicing. Here's a guide to the different types and the body benefits they provide (keep in mind, though, that many classes and even yoga videos often mix different styles into one session):

Ashtanga Yoga

This is the most vigorous form of yoga, as it involves doing yoga poses—standing, seated, back bends, and inversions (where a pose has you hold your head below the heart)—one after the other in rapid, flowing movements without much of a break. It also goes by names like Vinyasa, power, or power yoga. If you're looking for calorie burn, this is often the best option.

In one study, researchers from Long Island University and Columbia University compared an hour of beginner Ashtanga yoga with walking on the treadmill for twenty minutes. The study found that Ashtanga yoga offered some cardiovascular benefits, increasing the heart rate to the level of a moderate walk. Intermediate and advanced classes provide even more vigorous exercise, but researchers did note that all classes are different (so benefits can't be guaranteed across all classes) and that yoga shouldn't be a stand-in for other forms of heart-pumping exercise, which is important for cardiovascular health. (Ross, 2010; National Center for Complementary and Alternative Health, 2019; Newswise, 2015)

Bikram Yoga

This form of yoga is performed in a heated room (typically 105 degrees with 60 percent humidity), and it's often called hot yoga. Heat warms the muscles, allowing for greater flexibility and stretching. This is why Bikram yoga, which often runs through a series of twenty-six postures each performed twice during a ninety-minute session, has been found to be effective in increasing shoulder, back, and hamstring flexibility. (Bikram Yoga, 2019)

Hatha Yoga

This is one of the most popular forms of yoga and can also go by the names gentle yoga or restorative yoga. It involves slowly moving in and out of poses with controlled breathing. While not necessarily aerobic, hatha yoga does challenge almost every muscle in the body, particularly when you hold your poses for long periods of time. One study, published in the *International Journal of Yoga*, found that hatha yoga was better than aerobic exercise at improving balance, flexibility, and strength. (Hagins et al, 2007; Ross et al, 2010; Prado et al, 2014)

Iyengar Yoga

This type of yoga emphasizes physical alignment and makes use of bolsters, straps, blocks, blankets, and other props to help you get into the proper physical position. Iyengar can improve strength, stamina, balance, and flexibility. In one study, Swiss researchers found that people with chronic lower back pain who practiced Iyengar yoga had significantly less disability, pain, and depression after just six months.

Because they require you to lift your own body weight to balance, many yoga poses strengthen muscles and bones, too. Yoga also gets your blood flowing, helping to boost circulation. What's more, research from the National Institutes of Health found that regular yoga, no matter what kind, can prevent and even reverse the effects of chronic pain. While other forms of exercise may trigger pain, yoga goes beyond that and actually reverses pain. These are all reasons why yoga works for all ages and all fitness levels—and why yoga is an exercise that most people can do for a lifetime. (Crow et al, 2015; Bergland, 2015; Vallath, 2010)

Simple Stretching as Exercise

Yoga is one of the best ways to stretch and increase flexibility, but it's not the only way. Simple stretching at home can boost flexibility and range of motion, increase blood flow to the muscles and the brain, improve posture, and increase balance, which is so important as you get older. When done slowly and with gentle breathing, it's also an effective stress reliever. Simple stretches you can try at home include:

Downward Dog

This yoga move stretches legs, hips, back, and shoulders, and is an effective opening exercise for all seven chakras. Start in table pose, kneeling on all fours. Align knees under the hips and hands under the shoulders. Then push your hips up to the ceiling to form a "triangle" with the body. Keep your head between your arms and straighten your legs as much as possible. Maintain your position as long as you can, then come back down into table pose.

Gentle Neck Release

This gentle stretch opens up a tight neck area and helps to open the throat chakra. Sit in a chair with your feet flat on the ground. Place your right hand next to your right knee, while placing your left hand on top of your head. Gently tilt your head to the left. Return your head to upright position. Repeat this stretch on the other side.

Chest Opener

This movement helps opens up your shoulders and chest and your heart chakra. Reach both arms behind you, interlock your fingers, gently pull your shoulders back, and lift your arms.

Side Bend

This move stretches the back and sides and is important to do when you hunch over a desk or computer for long hours. It also helps open your solar plexus chakra. Stand up straight, feet together and arms overhead. Clasp hands together, interlacing fingers and extending the pointer fingers to the ceiling. Slowly bend your upper body to the left while you breathe out. Hold for a count of five breaths. Slowly come back to center and repeat on the other side.

Butterfly

This stretch helps open your sacral chakra and your groin area. Sit on the floor, knees bent out to your sides, with the soles of your feet touching. Pull your feet gently toward your body.

Quad Stretch

This movement stretches the quadriceps or muscles on the front part of the legs, while helping to open your root chakra. Stand arm's length away from a wall, while your left hand touches the wall. Bend your right knee, bringing your foot up behind you. Then grab your right foot with your right hand. Hold stretch for ten to twelve seconds, then switch to the other side.

Important Stretching Tips

Don't force any movement. If you feel pain, stop there. Never push beyond the point where you feel comfortable. Over time, you'll be able to do deeper stretches as your muscles become more flexible. But for now, if you force a movement, you'll end up pulling a muscle and getting hurt.

Breathe into your stretch. Slow, gentle breathing in and out while you're stretching will help calm your mind and relax your body. The more relaxed you are, the less tense your muscles and the deeper you'll be able to stretch.

Keep your arms and legs bent slightly while stretching. This will help you avoid pulling a muscle while stretching.

Aim to stretch for about ten to fifteen minutes, three to four days a week. If you want to incorporate it into your daily routine, plan to stretch every night before bed. Light a candle or some incense or play soft relaxing music to help create a nighttime ritual that will relax you even more and help you to sleep more soundly.

Strength Training How-To

Aerobic exercise works the heart, which is a muscle. It also burns calories and fat. But strength training builds muscle, which boosts your bone strength and your resting metabolism, helping you burn more calories while you're at rest. The more muscle you have, the more calories you'll burn all day long. Also, the more muscle you have, the stronger your bones. These are good reasons to consistently include both cardiovascular exercise or aerobic exercise and strength training in your routine.

Strength training or weight-bearing exercise—using weights in the gym, doing body-weight exercises like push-ups, or doing strengthening poses in yoga or Pilates—is essential to building stronger bones. Here's how it works: cells called osteoblasts are critical to maintaining your bone structure. When you do weight-bearing exercise, you're stressing your bones in a good way. Each time you stress your bones, the osteoblasts lay down new bone tissue to strengthen the areas where the bone is stressed. Do regular strength training for different parts of the body and the osteoblasts continue to reinforce the bone, over and over again. (Layne et al, 1999; Harvard Health Publishing, 2019; Berkeley Wellness, 2019)

To get started, first check with your doctor to be sure you are able to do strength training without complications. Once you get your doctor's okay, do some sort of aerobic activity for five to ten minutes to warm up the muscles, helping to prevent injury. Then choose a weight or resistance level that will tire your muscles after twelve repetitions. (When you can do more than fifteen reps without tiring, increase the amount of weight or resistance.) Plan to do two or three twenty- to thirty-minute sessions a week.

Some easy ways to add strength training to your routine:

- **Wear a walking vest.** These adjustable weighted vests can be worn daily to transform your daily walks into strength-training ones.

- **Do body weight exercises.** Push-ups are the easiest exercises to do. You don't need any equipment and can do them anywhere. Start with one push-up a day and eventually add another and then another. Other good options include squats for your legs and crunches for your abs. These can be done at home before you shower in the morning or while you're watching TV. One idea: whenever there's a commercial break, do a couple. It's an easy way to fit in strength training.

- **Try resistance tubes.** These stretchy, lightweight pieces of latex provide resistance and strength training when stretched. (The lighter the color of the tubing, the less resistance it offers.) You can do a variety of moves with these anywhere. I keep one at my desk at work for quick arm exercises during the day, in between patients. I find Instagram,

Pinterest, and YouTube great sources of moves and videos for different exercise equipment, including resistance tubes.

- **Do free weights or try the weight machines at the gym.** Dumbbells are effective strength training tools. You can do things like bicep curls to strengthen the arms and shoulder raises to strengthen the shoulders, as well as weighted squats to help boost muscle and bone in the legs. Weight machines at the gym are a more advanced way to build strength. I always recommend talking to a trainer first to learn how to use them so you don't injure yourself.

Exercise and Your Health

Not only does exercise boost the mind, it also has tremendous benefits for the body and your long-term health. First and foremost, exercise has been shown to help you live longer. Researchers have consistently found that even a little bit of regular exercise has big benefits when it comes to your health. In one study, researchers at the University of Oxford in the United Kingdom found that being physically active a few times per week was enough to lower risks of heart disease, stroke, and blood clots. Another study from the University of Utah found that just moving for two minutes every hour instead of being sedentary was associated with longevity and, more specifically, with a 33 percent lower risk of dying overall. This means just getting up from your desk or chair every hour for two minutes to take a walk around your office, go up and down a set of stairs, or take a quick walk outside and back is enough to prolong your life.

There are many reasons for this boost in longevity. The first is that exercise keeps your heart healthy. We so often forget that the heart is a muscle and, like other muscles in the body, you have to move it or lose it. A stronger heart is a healthier heart. Exercise also helps the heart in other ways, according to research published in the journal *Circulation*:

- You lose weight when you get moving. Excess weight puts undue strain on the heart, so losing weight is better for the heart.

- Physical activity helps reduce overall cholesterol, which has been linked to clogged arteries, and LDL (or "bad") cholesterol levels in the blood, which contribute to heart disease. It also raises HDL (or "good") cholesterol levels in the blood.

- Regular exercise promotes lower blood pressure. High blood pressure strains the heart and can lead to chest pain and heart attacks.

- Moving regularly improves the body's ability to use insulin to control glucose levels in the blood, a risk factor for diabetes, which is also a risk factor for heart disease.

- It improves the ability of the blood vessels to dilate, which results in improved oxygen flow to the body, the muscles, and the heart.

- By exercising regularly, you can also reduce the number of hormones circulating in the body. Excess hormones in the body have been linked to diseases like breast cancer. By reducing your weight, you're also helping to reduce the amount of estrogen in the bloodstream. Fat cells are able to produce estrogen; the more weight you're carrying, the more estrogen circulating in your body and the higher your risk of diseases like cancer. As we get older, our body holds on to these estrogen-producing fat cells, making it harder to lose weight without exercise. (University of Utah, 2015; Cornell University, 2002)

- Exercise, particularly moderate exercise, has also been shown in studies, like one from the University of Illinois, to keep your immune system strong, helping you stay free from sickness. This moderate type of exercise (think walking, gardening, and dancing) is the kind practiced by the Ikarians, which is even more proof of its health-boosting effects. Exercise, both aerobic and strength training, is also essential for boosting muscle and bone. German researchers found that after the age of forty, up to 50 percent of muscle mass can be lost (a condition called sarcopenia), resulting in weakness and reduced ability to carry out everyday tasks. This is just one reason why regular and consistent exercise is critical as we get older. (Mann et al, 2014; Reynolds, 2009; Martin et al, 2009; Dennison et al, 2015; Keller et al, 2013)

- It helps you sleep better. Another reason moving your body has such a big impact on your health: it helps you fall asleep more quickly, sleep longer, and have an overall better quality of sleep than you would before exercising. It's during sleep that the body rejuvenates and repairs, something that I'll discuss more in the next chapter. (Dolezal et al, 2017; ScienceDirect, 2011; National Sleep Foundation, 2019)

The Body: A Potent Detoxer

The kidneys, the liver, the digestive tract, and the lymphatic system (a network of vessels and organs that run parallel to the cardiovascular system and are part of the immune system) all play a critical role in eliminating toxins that we're exposed to on a daily basis—pollution, pesticides, and processed foods, for example. The body also produces cellular waste that needs to be removed as well. Lactic acid, produced by the muscles during exercise, is one example. Your cells also produce cellular waste products if your body is fighting a virus or infection or is under a great deal of stress.

In order to effectively detox, though, you need to be sure you're drinking enough water before and after exercise. Drinking water (around eight, 8-ounce glasses daily) is important any time of the day because we're composed mainly of water. Without enough water, the body can't rid itself of toxins through the liver and kidneys, which are responsible for flushing waste from the body. This is why staying hydrated before and after exercise is even more important. Consider all this detoxification the body's way of housecleaning.

Put all these pieces together and regular, consistent exercise throughout your life will help you live a longer, happier, disease-free life. Add exercise along with a Mediterranean diet, and you've got a longevity combination that is a win-win for your health.

The Importance of the Breath

Breathing properly is one of the central parts of any relaxation exercise, and likewise, it's one of the essential aspects of exercising in general. Whether you're doing yoga (when slow, relaxed diaphragmatic breaths are key) or running (when rhythmic breathing is important), the breath is what brings in the oxygen to fuel your brain and muscles. It's what gives you the ability to sustain exercise. The more you move, the more oxygen your body requires. Slow, controlled breathing while stretching can also allow the muscles to relax so you can deepen your stretch while calming the mind. Shallow breathing, on the other hand, doesn't allow the body to get enough oxygen. This can intensify feelings of anxiety as well as increasing blood pressure and heart rate.

Why Exercise Is Good for Your Skin

When you exercise, you boost circulation, sending blood with its oxygen and key nutrients to all cells in the body, including the skin cells. This increase in nutrient-rich blood flow gives us a healthy, radiant, post-workout glow. This boost in circulation also helps carry away waste products from skin cells and all working cells, helping to flush them out of the system.

Researchers from McMaster University in Ontario also found that regular exercise may also help reverse skin aging and keep the skin youthful looking. The study volunteers who exercised at least three hours a week (with moderate or vigorous physical activity) had a healthier stratum corneum, the outermost layer of the epidermis, and a thicker dermal layer. The dermis is the second layer of skin, where connective tissue like collagen and elastin—the structural proteins that keep the firm skin and elastic—are found. What's more, the forty-year-old exercisers had skin that was much younger looking and was similar to that of twenty- and thirty-year-olds. One theory of the researchers is that exercise causes the release of substances called myokines, which trigger healthy changes in cells. Exercisers had almost 50 percent more myokines in their skin than they did at the start of the study. (Reynolds, 2014)

How Much Exercise Is Enough?

This is a question that many patients ask me when we're discussing the importance of exercise. I believe that just moving your body as much as you can is helpful. But people often like a "prescription" for exercise, specifically how much they should exercise every day and every week. First, I always recommend that they check with their primary care doctor before engaging in any form of exercise to be sure that their body, and their heart, can handle what they're doing.

I agree, though, with what researchers recommend. Most of the studies showing the positive effects of exercising use a guideline of thirty to sixty minutes of continuous exercise three to five days per week. The intensity of your exercise should be 60 percent to 75 percent of your max heart rate. (This basically tells you how much you should be exercising based on your age.) To determine your max heart rate, subtract your age from 220. If you're forty-five, your maximum heart rate is 175 and 60 percent of that is a heart rate of 105 beats per minute. Seventy-five percent is a heart rate of 131 beats per minute. If you're using a heart rate monitor, it should register between 105 and 131 beats for heart-healthy benefits.

If you exercise too hard (over your maximum heart rate), you're straining, which is bad for your heart. That's a sign that you need to slow down. If it's too low, you're not challenging your heart muscle enough to gain real benefits.

Making Exercise Fit into Your Busy Life

We all live very busy lives, making it hard to fit in everything we need to do, including exercise. Without exercise, however, all the other parts of the healthy beauty and longevity equation don't work synergistically, so exercise is one part you can't skip. Here are some tips that my patients have shared with me about how they find the time for exercise in their schedules.

- **Do what you love.** If you hate running, don't tell yourself you have to get to the gym to run on the treadmill. That's a sure reason why you'll skip the gym any chance you get. Find something you love to do and then go out and do it.

Haven't found your movement love yet? Explore and try new things. You'll find something, even a workout class you never thought you'd like, but ends up being a passion. Once you find that passion, you'll find yourself wanting to exercise and looking forward to it.

- **Fit movement into your daily life.** Finding ways to fit in movement is easier if you incorporate it into things you're already doing: walk to the library or park instead of driving, park at the end of the grocery parking lot and walk back and forth rather than snagging the closest spot, take the stairs instead of the elevator, do gardening or yard work, fit in some jumping jacks while you're waiting for dinner to cook, or vacuum the living room or house. Add some of your favorite mood-boosting music to kick-start your energy.

- **Walk your way healthy.** Sometimes, one of the most enjoyable activities is to lace up your walking shoes and just get outdoors in your neighborhood after dinner, on weekends at the local park, or on a beautiful trail out of town. If you do no other activity, just walking for at least thirty minutes every day will rev up your heart rate, while you breathe in fresh air and clear your mind. According to the American Heart Association, you can reap plenty of health benefits from walking, including lowering your risk of heart disease, enhancing mental well-being, and reducing your risk of osteoporosis, cancer, and type 2 diabetes. (American Heart Association, 2019)

- **Mark it on your schedule,** as you would a meeting or a big event. We schedule meetings and can't cancel them. Exercise is just as important because it's critical to your health and your life. Book it, make it non-negotiable, and you'll have a better chance of doing it more regularly.

- Establish goals. Figure out what you hope to gain from exercise (e.g., weight loss, improved health, reduced anxiety) and write it down, so when your motivation is waning, you can look at this and have renewed inspiration.

- **Change things up.** Even if you love what you do, if you do it day in and day out, you'll get bored. It happens to even the most motivated among us. Change the course you're walking or running on, and mix up your workout throughout the week. I personally find that keeping an exercise video or two at home helps you to mix things up, particularly if you're crunched for time. I always keep these videos (including yoga videos) around for those days when I don't have time to drive to the gym—or it's just too cold to go outside, which happens often during the winter months. One of my favorites is a quick twenty-five minute full body workout; it's perfect for time-crunched days because it's fast and effective!

- **Do just five minutes if that's all the time you have.** You'll feel better having done something, and who knows, you may want to keep going after that.

Our bodies are meant to move, just as they're meant to eat healthy foods. Do your body a favor, get out there and exercise. You definitely won't regret it.

Where Do You Go from Here?

We've talked so much about de-stressing and finding your spiritual center, eating the right foods, and moving your body. It's time to move on to the next step for a healthier, more beautiful you: sleep. It's absolutely critical for your health and your skin. You'll find out just why it's so important for you, and how to get better sleep, in the upcoming chapter.

CHAPTER 5

SLEEP BETTER AND MORE SOUNDLY

THINK ABOUT A TIME when you didn't get enough sleep—either you went to bed way too late or you just couldn't fall or stay asleep. The next day you were tired and groggy and probably reaching for more sugar and caffeine to keep your eyes open and your energy levels up. Maybe you were too tired to exercise. And most likely your skin had a dullness to it as well. Your spirit and sense of self possibly even felt worn down too.

All the healthy habits you've put into place thus far are usually the first things out the window after a sleepless night. We've all been there.

One or two sleepless nights here or there is to be expected with all that we're juggling today. But what's becoming all too common is the overwhelming insomnia and consistent lack of quality, restful sleep night after night that people are experiencing today. In fact, an estimated fifty to seventy million people in the US today experience what's called a "sleep or wakefulness disorder," according to the National Institutes of Health. (Colton et al, 2006)

Researchers spend millions of dollars trying to figure out why people can't sleep and how to fix the pervasive insomnia in our society. The main reason, however, that people can't get enough sleep has everything to do with our lifestyle. Think back to the simple Ikarian lifestyles we've talked about throughout this book. Every day, these centenarians get plenty of fresh air, nutritious food, regular exercise outdoors, and daily companionship through friends and family. They also don't have a lot of stress and if they do get stressed, it's pretty short lived. They're not "glued" to their phones 24/7, checking work emails or sitting in offices until late in the evening, anxious about meeting a work deadline.

Their simple lives may not be realistic with the rhythms or dictates of a modern work-oriented society, but their lives work synergistically with the natural rhythms of the human body. They nap during the day if they're tired, and when night comes, they eat a light dinner (something that's directly opposed to an American style of eating) and go to bed. And when they go to bed, they sleep easily and soundly with little interruption.

Our work-life patterns are competing with the natural rhythms of our bodies, keeping us awake at night and groggy during the day. And even if you say you function great on just four hours of sleep a night, your body is keeping track when it comes to your health. Long-term, you may pay the price in terms of chronic disease and longevity. This is not meant to scare you. It's only meant to give you the information you need to create the life and the health you want and that your body craves. You need sleep to keep your body, your brain, and your skin healthy. Sleep is also essential for our spiritual selves. In a society where the need to sleep is seen almost as a weakness, relinquishing our bodies to slumber is surrendering to its natural rhythms. Honoring that and getting the rest we need allows us to see things more clearly and to be more in tune with our spirits.

If you're taking a pill to help you fall, and stay, asleep (as almost nine million Americans do), you're not relinquishing control of your body. You are controlling when the body sleeps and wakes, which is not good for your health or your spirit. Allowing your body's natural day-night rhythm (referred to as circadian rhythm) to get into sync on its own is so important. It's your circadian rhythm that acts as your internal sleep/wake clock. It controls when you feel sleepy and when you feel energized and awake. It cycles based on the twenty-four-hour rhythms of nature; when the eyes see light after the sun rises and dark after the sun sets. It works most efficiently when you have regular sleep/wake habits. The hypothalamus in the brain controls this clock, and therefore controls the release of the sleep hormone melatonin. Having enough of this hormone makes you fall asleep.

Your circadian rhythm does more than just affect your sleep, however. It affects the release of hormones in the body, body temperature, eating habits, and digestion. This is why having a circadian rhythm that's out of sync has been linked to chronic health conditions like obesity, diabetes, and depression. Having a regular sleep/wake cycle can help prevent these conditions and keep you healthy.

Take a sleeping pill and you're forcing your body into slumber without fixing the reasons why it can't sleep in the first place. Short term, it seems great: you're sleeping and you feel energized during the day. But long term, these pills, both prescription and non-prescription, can wreak havoc on your natural circadian rhythm as well as your body and your mind. Researchers from Canada and

France found that over-the-counter sleep aids and certain antihistamines used to promote sleep increase a person's risk of developing dementia and Alzheimer's disease. (DailyNews, 2013; Time, 2014; Medical News Today, 2015)

Why Your Body Needs Sleep

There's a reason it's nicknamed "beauty sleep." Restful sleep makes a huge difference in the health of the body, as well as in the health and radiance of the skin. Matthew is a patient of mine who is prone to outbreaks of the herpes simplex virus around his lips, which causes cold sores. I know immediately when he comes in with an outbreak that he's been working around the clock and hasn't been sleeping. Then there's Alyson, another patient of mine. She has eczema, something we're able to keep under control when she's eating right, exercising regularly, and getting enough sleep. As soon as her lifestyle gets hectic, as it often does for this financial executive, the eczema flares up. Ditto for my patients with alopecia areata (hair loss), psoriasis, and acne.

This quote from Thomas Dekker says it all: "Sleep is the golden chain that ties health and our bodies together." Sleep keeps us healthy and keeps our minds sharp. In children and teens, it's during sleep that growth and development primarily occurs. It's during sleep that the body does its repair work. It's when the body's energy supplies, depleted during the day, are restored. It's during sleep when muscle tissue is rebuilt and restored. And it's also during sleep that growth hormones, critical for rebuilding tissue, are secreted.

As one preeminent sleep expert, Neil B. Kavey, has said, "Think of the body as a car. No car can keep going and going and going without a tune-up or oil change. If it's not tuned, the car may keep running, but not as smoothly as it did when it was maintained properly. You can think of sleep as your body's daily tune-up.

"Human beings can function without a full tune-up, but they will be in a state of relative sleep deprivation and won't be able to work or to think as well as they do when they are fully rested. It's like an engine that gets only four out of eight spark plugs replaced and then runs sluggishly."

Sleep is essential for just about every single process that occurs in the body. More specifically, it does the following:

- **Sleep keeps your brain sharp.** Sleep is critical for normal functioning of the brain, says research from Oxford University. According to sleep scientists, sleep serves as the "brain's housekeeper," helping to restore and repair the brain. Poor sleep over time, they found, causes brain shrinkage and problems with reasoning, planning, memory, and problem-solving. In fact, one study published in the journal *Sleep* found that losing just half a night of shut-eye makes memories less accessible in stressful situations. (Haelle, 2014; Cedernaes et al, 2015)

  This all makes perfect sense. It's during sleep that your brain forms new pathways to help you learn and absorb new information. (This is why it's often recommended that you rest after you've learned something new, in school or after learning a new skill.) European researchers found that sleep helps us focus and remember information often by the strengthening of neural connections that form our memories.

  But all aspects of sleep are important for the brain. Researchers at the University of California found that rapid eye movement sleep, or REM sleep (a stage of sleep during which dreaming most frequently occurs) plays an important role in learning new information. Deep, restorative sleep is also important because this is when the brain processes and consolidates newly acquired information. (Rasch et al, 2013; ScienceDaily, 2015; Harvard Medical School, 2007; McDevitt et al, 2015; Barry, 2011)

• **Enough sleep also helps us make better decisions** (our judgment is impaired without enough restful slumber). We're better able to assess a situation, plan accordingly, and choose the correct behavior. Without enough sleep, we're not focused, we're less attentive, and we're less likely to learn and process facts. These are all good reasons to get more zzzs.

• **Sleep keeps your heart healthy.** Lack of sleep is a risk factor for cardiovascular disease, along with a poor diet, lack of exercise, and smoking. Research published in the *European Journal of Preventive Cardiology* found that not getting enough shut-eye is linked to heart attacks and strokes. In fact, the researchers found that nearly 63 percent of their study participants who had a heart attack also had a sleeping disorder. They found that those with sleeping disorders had up to four times higher risk of stroke than those who got enough sleep. (Godman, 2014; European Society of Cardiology, 2015; ScienceDaily, 2017)

• **Sleep makes you happier.** Not getting enough sleep can affect your mood, making you more tense, more nervous, and more irritable. Chronic insomnia may also increase the risk of developing depression or an anxiety disorder. Having a negative mood can impact relationships at work, at home, and with friends and family, contributing to stress and unhappiness. (Oginska et al, 2006)

In fact, a group of researchers in Sweden found that not getting enough sleep contributes to higher job stress levels, a feeling of loss of control at work, and more emotional overreactions on the job. I would venture a guess that these results hold true for everything in our lives outside of work, too. If you're not sleeping and not loving your job, your relationships, or other aspects of your life, it's important to try to solve your sleep issues before making any big decisions. Getting enough sleep can help you see things more clearly, something you can't do when you're fatigued day in and day out. (Akerstedt et al, 2015)

The sleep-stress cycle can go round and round, as I see with so many of my patients. Having more tension and anxiety (often from work) can keep you up at night, creating a never-ending cycle of sleep loss. Get enough sleep on a regular basis and your feelings and mood will stabilize, as will your outlook on life.

- **Sleep keeps you at a healthy weight.** There have been numerous studies done on the effects of the lack of sleep on weight. One study, conducted by researchers in Qatar, found that losing just thirty minutes of sleep per night can cause you to gain weight and affect both insulin resistance and your metabolism, slowing it down. Other research, published in the journal *Proceedings of the National Academy of Sciences* or *PNAS*, found that sleeping less than five hours a night is associated with cravings for more and higher-calorie, carbohydrate-rich foods, triggering weight gain. In fact, research has shown that people eat, on average, about 300 calories more per day when they're tired. Anyone who's ever been tired doesn't need research to confirm this. (Patel et al, 2006; Markwald et al, 2013)

But why do you gain weight when you're tired, besides the fact that you're eating more sweets and treats? Research shows that fatigue-triggered weight gain has everything to do with hormones, which seem to go haywire when you don't get enough shut-eye. Remember it's your circadian rhythm that controls the release of hormones. Losing just a few hours of sleep a few nights in a row is enough to trigger immediate weight gain. This sleep deprivation increases levels of a hormone called ghrelin, which intensifies cravings and hunger, and lowers levels of a hormone called leptin, which is the hormone that tells you to stop eating because you're full or satiated. What this means: when you're sleep deprived, you're less likely to resist the urge to eat unhealthy junk food.

Getting enough sleep also keeps your metabolism— your fat-burning furnace—stoked, which can help you from gaining weight. A team of researchers at the University of South Carolina and Arizona State University found that metabolism can be slowed even when you lose just two critical hours of sleep three nights in a row. Add this to your carbohydrate cravings and you've got a surefire recipe for weight gain. (Hellmich, 2014; Newswise, 2015)

- **Sleep helps you live longer.** Sleep deprivation (even just one night) has been linked to biological aging. Research from the University of California-San Diego found that women who get five hours or less of sleep a night don't live as long as women who get, on average, 6.5 to 7.5 hours of sleep a night. Keep in mind that every body is different. What may work for some (i.e., five hours a night) won't work for others. (American Academy of Sleep Medicine, 2015)

One study, published in the journal *Diabetes Care*, also found that *too* much sleep, particularly for people with weight problems, could be a risk factor for type 2 diabetes. This makes sense. Spend too much time in bed and not enough time moving around and you could be at risk for even more health problems than just diabetes. The key is moderation, as it is with eating, exercise, work, and just about everything in life, and finding what works best for *your* body. (MPR, 2015)

- **Sleep helps curb inflammation.** Inflammation, as I mentioned earlier in this book, is linked to everything from heart disease to premature aging. But studies show that lack of sleep, specifically six or fewer hours a night, triggers high blood levels of inflammatory proteins. A team of Boston-based doctors also reported, in one study, that one marker of inflammation, called C-reactive protein, is actually higher in people who get six or fewer hours of sleep every night. This is the protein that's linked to a greater risk of heart problems. (Mullington et al, 2010)

- **Sleep helps you perform better physically.** A Stanford University School of Medicine study found that college basketball players who slept at least ten hours a night for five to seven weeks ran faster, improved shooting accuracy, and improved overall game performance. But you don't have to be a star basketball player to reap the benefits of sleep. These same study findings can be extrapolated to your everyday physical performance, even if it's just how far you're able to walk in the morning or how you perform in a local 5K. (Stanford Medicine News Center, 2011)

- **Sleep reduces stress.** Get enough sleep and whatever is triggering your anxiety just won't seem that insurmountable anymore. Sleeping gives the body a chance to relax and rest without being overwhelmed by worry. The opposite is true, too. Lack of sleep increases anxiety and stress. One study, published in the journal *Sleep*, found that tossing and turning just one night was enough to increase levels of stress hormones like cortisol by the very next evening. And after just one night of sleep deprivation, people also had an increase in levels of norepinephrine, a key hormone and neurotransmitter that increases the body's heart rate, blood pressure, and blood sugar in response to stress. Prolonged periods of shortened sleep increase a person's blood pressure and heart rate at night, two major risk factors for heart disease. Experience sleep loss night after night and your stress levels—including levels of stress hormones and ACTH, the chemical messenger in the body that tells the adrenal gland to release even more stress hormones—skyrocket. (Woolston, 2015; Leproult et al, 1997)

I've found that just the thought of not sleeping is all it takes to cause patients to develop enough anxiety to not sleep again the following night. And the cycle repeats itself over and over until patients come in to see me about a particular skin condition that's gotten worse and I find out they haven't gotten a good night's sleep in weeks or sometimes months! In these cases, I give my patients this mantra to repeat to reduce the stress they're feeling: "I can get plenty of sleep every night and my body appreciates how I take care of it."

By getting enough sleep at night, the body is able to take a break from the stress hormones of the day, giving it a chance to relax and rejuvenate itself.

- **Sleep increases pain tolerance.** It turns out that people who have insomnia or other sleep disturbances also have increased sensitivity to pain. A team of Norwegian researchers found that a reduced tolerance to pain was 52 percent higher in those people who report having insomnia more than once weekly. They're not sure the reason why, but these sleep scientists theorize that a neurotransmitter called dopamine, which plays a role in many functions including movement, memory, attention/focus, problem-solving, anxiety, and pain processing, may be affected by the lack of sleep. (Newswise, 2015; Sivertsen et al, 2015)

- **Sleep boosts the immune system.** Getting adequate amounts of sleep keeps the immune system functioning properly. In one study, researchers from the Netherlands and the United Kingdom found that a lack of sleep caused a reduction in the number of white blood cells called granulocytes, which are critical to immune function. Just one night of sleep deprivation also lowers levels of something called interleukin-6, an antiviral protein that's critical to immune system functioning. These are two reasons, researchers theorize, why a lack of sleep contributes to illness and chronic diseases like diabetes. (Medical News Today, 2012; Newswise, 2019)

Another study, published in the journal *Sleep*, found that those people who averaged between seven and eight hours of sleep a night were sick less often. What this means: when you get enough sleep, along with eating healthy, meditating, and exercising, you'll rarely get sick. But lose a couple nights of sleep to a busy schedule and you can easily catch the cold that's being passed around. (Medical News Today, 2012; Newswise, 2019; ScienceDaily, 2014)

- **Sleep also improves your skin.** Not only do you feel and think better after getting a restful night of sleep, you also look better. Sleep scientists at the University of California-Irvine found that when your circadian clock is out of sync, skin aging, including fine lines and wrinkles, roughness and dryness, and dull skin is accelerated, as is your risk of skin cancer. This is a pretty compelling argument to get enough shut-eye every night. (ScienceDaily, 2015)

How to Get a Good Night's Sleep

You know all the reasons why sleep is so critical for the body, but now how do you get to sleep, particularly when you've got so much going on during the day and in your mind at night? This is a topic I regularly discuss with my patients, as it's such a critical part of a balanced lifestyle. Here are some of the sleep-better tips that get results for my patients.

- **Move your body every day.** Study after study shows that physical activity during the day helps you fall asleep more quickly at night, sleep longer, and have overall better sleep quality. This research comes as no surprise to me. Moving the body, which is what we're biologically designed to do, helps tire us out, particularly if we're outdoors in the fresh air. One group of researchers found that 150 minutes of exercise every week (about twenty minutes of exercise per day) helps people sleep more soundly at night and feel more alert during the day. Another group of researchers from the University of Pennsylvania found that certain types of exercise, what they call "purposeful" activity—that is, activity that promotes an end goal—promote sleep better than others. This includes walking, biking, yoga, running, weight lifting, and even gardening. This is the type of activity that the Ikarians make a point to do every day. (National Sleep Foundation, 2019; Mental Health and Physical Activity, 2011; Newswise, 2015)

Be cautious about exercising right before bedtime, however, unless you're doing gentle, relaxing yoga stretches or rhythmic tai chi. Vigorous aerobic exercise before bedtime boosts circulation and could end up revving you up and keeping you awake at night.

- **Eat a light dinner.** The Ikarians, and even Mediterranean people today, eat their heaviest meals early in the day, saving their lightest meals for evening. Soup, vegetables, and salads with a slice of whole grain bread are common meals in the evening, not the large-portioned heavy dinners that are so common in America. If you eat too much, your body spends most of its energy digesting food at night when it should be relaxing. These heavy meals can interfere with restful sleep.

- **Create a consistent sleep schedule that works for your life.** A set bedtime, when you can realistically go to bed every night based on your work, your family, and your life, is a must. Consistency is important for proper functioning of your circadian rhythm. It helps your body to understand when it's time for sleep.

  Your sleep schedule might even include nighttime rituals like meditation to help relax you and your thoughts, reading a paper (not electronic) book, giving yourself a gentle massage, and/or having a cup of herbal (not caffeinated) tea. Rituals are important because they help prepare the body and mind for sleep.

  For this reason, it's also important to have a set wake time every day even on weekends. Regularly sleeping in or catching up on sleep on weekends throws off your circadian rhythm and may affect how well you sleep as you get back into your work week.

- **Keep your room cool.** Rooms that are too hot or too cold can make you feel uncomfortable and can disturb your sleep. The ideal temperature, say experts, is 65°F, but what's important is to find a temperature that's most comfortable for you. I find that a temperature around 70°F is best for me. Having the right humidity levels in your bedroom is also important, particularly during cold weather months. If a room is too dry, you won't breathe as easily, which can interfere with your slumber. Buying a simple humidifier and running it until humidity levels reach between 40 and 50 percent can help. Just remember to regularly clean and disinfect it with distilled white vinegar so bacteria don't build up inside the water reservoir. (Heid, 2014)

- **Shut down electronics at night.** Don't leave your phone or your computer by your bed. (If you need an alarm clock, use a battery-powered one instead.) Set your screensaver to "night shift," "night time," or "night light" (there are various names for the same type of settings). These will change the color of your screen at certain times of the day to help you sleep better at night. (Stonybrook University, 2014)

Study after study has found that the blue light that emanates from electronics, your TV, your computer, your smartphone, and your e-reader can affect your circadian rhythms. Every one of us has something called photoreceptors in our eyes that register and process light before sending it to the brain. The brain reacts to blue light by suppressing the production of melatonin because this light mimics the wavelengths of natural daylight. It's melatonin that's released as darkness sets in at night. The more melatonin we have in our system, the sleepier we get. Our body starts to repress the production of melatonin once the sun starts to rise in the morning, so we can wake up and not feel groggy. It's melatonin that controls sleep and wake cycles and is essential to our circadian rhythm. (de la Iglesia et al, 2015)

Blue light, which is omnipresent in our households and work environments, is confusing the brain and our circadian rhythm about whether we should be awake or asleep. The result is persistent sleeplessness and insomnia, which many people try to "fix" by taking sleep medications. (Holzman, 2010)

By shutting off your devices before bed, you may find that you fall asleep more quickly and stay asleep longer. One

University of Colorado study, done with campers out in the wilderness with no exposure to any artificial light including the blue light emanating from electronics, found that the campers slept longer and more soundly without exposure to lights than they did when not camping. And we don't need a study to know that the Ikarians don't use smartphones and computers all day long. The bottom line is this: health starts with maintaining a synchronized circadian rhythm.

• **Find ways to relax.** Stress and anxiety are pervasive in our modern society and are key reasons people have trouble sleeping. Meditation, sitting quietly at night and just deeply breathing, taking a short nighttime stroll outdoors, and/ or avoiding the news right before bedtime (which is a big source of stress) are all good ways to power down the body and the mind before sleep. Everyone is different, so experiment to see what works best for you and put it into regular practice.

• **Take a power nap, if you can.** One thing the people of Ikaria know is the benefits of an afternoon nap. This is part of their daily lives and may be just one reason why they tend to live so long. It turns out that the Ikarians are on to something. Taking just a short "power" nap during the day, particularly when you're sleepy, has the power to restore you and your health. One study, conducted in Paris, found that a short, thirty-minute nap can restore hormones to their normal levels, reducing stress and boosting the immune system. Napping, say the researchers, gives the body a chance to recover from the effects of sleeplessness, which is key to maintaining health.

How, though, do you fit in a nap in a busy day? It's not easy, but it's not impossible either. If you have an office, shut the door and your eyes during your lunch hour, but set the timer on your computer or phone so you wake up after thirty minutes. You may not even really sleep. You may just be in a state of resting wakefulness, which is relaxing too. If you don't have an office or a lounge, take your lunch hour a little later and just get outside to walk in nature for thirty minutes. The fresh air and quiet will rejuvenate your mind, body, and spirit as well, and help you sleep better at night. (Newswise, 2019)

- **Be sure you're getting enough vitamin D.** If you're having trouble sleeping, it might be a good idea to have your vitamin D levels checked by your primary care doctor. A deficiency of this vitamin has been linked to sleep problems. If you're deficient, you can try eating more vitamin D-rich foods like fatty fish (such as salmon), fortified milk or orange juice, or certain types of mushrooms that have been exposed to ultraviolet light (mushrooms produce vitamin D when exposed to light). These mushrooms are usually labeled as such on their packaging. Or, on the advice of your doctor, you may want to take a vitamin D_3 supplement. (*Sleep*, 2019)

Melatonin and Your Skin

The sleep hormone melatonin also turns out to have beneficial effects on the skin. Have enough of it in your body (one benefit of having a healthy sleep-wake cycle) and you may experience added protection from the sun's ultraviolet rays. Melatonin acts as an antioxidant, helping to suppress UV damage to exposed skin cells. This doesn't mean that getting enough sleep or having enough melatonin in your body eliminates your need for daily sunscreen (more on this in the next chapter). It just means that melatonin offers additional protection for your skin.

Having enough melatonin in your body also allows the skin to have a healthier stress response. Because melatonin is a free-radical scavenger and a broad-spectrum antioxidant it seems to help moderate the effects of stress, both external and internal, on the skin. This could, in turn, help reduce the skin problems that develop as a result of stress, like rough, dry skin and fine lines and wrinkles.

One downside of melatonin, however, is that in some people, it seems to activate the skin's pigment-producing cells called melanocytes, which can darken the skin. This is a reason why I don't recommend taking melatonin supplements to help you get to sleep. (Slominski et al, 2005)

The Five Healthy Stages of Sleep

In ancient times, darkness came and people went to sleep. They woke with the dawn to start their days. Doing so helped them honor their internal body clock, which ensured the proper production of the sleep hormone melatonin. Production of the stress hormone cortisol naturally lowers at night, gradually increasing throughout the night to help promote alertness in the morning.

Aligning our body clocks to modern society is hard to do. Many people are just getting out of work when it's dark and others work night shifts, which is wreaking havoc on our sleep patterns and our health. Getting enough melatonin, however, allows for the five healthy stages of sleep. Going through all five stages (one full sleep cycle) four to six times a night allows for truly restful, health-promoting sleep.

These five stages of healthy sleep are:

Stage 1: the lightest stage of sleep, when you feel yourself drifting off. It usually lasts for five to ten minutes. This is also typically the last stage of sleep before you wake up, if you wake up naturally (without an alarm clock).

Stage 2: the stage when brain activity slows down, as does body temperature. It lasts for about twenty minutes.

Stage 3: the start of deep sleep and typically when blood pressure drops, breathing slows down, and muscles become relaxed. (It's sometimes combined with stage 4 in discussions of sleep.) Stages 3 and 4 can last, together, for about an hour, though it takes up less time as you move through the cycles throughout the night.

Stage 4: the stage when you experience the deepest and most refreshing sleep. This is when the brain is the most relaxed, when the body does its repair work and rejuvenation, and when blood supply to the muscles increases and growth hormones are released. It's also a time when our conscious mind and our body are resting and our spiritual self is undergoing a restorative awakening and renewal. In India's ancient Upanishads, a collection of fundamental spiritual teachings that are central to Hinduism, it's this stage of deep sleep that offers "a deep state of utter peace wherein Awareness rests unto Awareness, without any egoic sense of body, mind, or world." This stage of sleep is when we let go of the body, mind, ego, plans, and concerns and are free in deeply peaceful contentedness. This may be why the Dalai Lama calls sleep "the best form of meditation." In fact, some believe that it's during deep sleep that our conscious selves leave the body to reconnect with our higher selves. It's why this stage of restorative sleep some people believe is the most important for body, mind, and spiritual restoration each night. (Enlightened Spirituality, 2019)

Stage 5: called active sleep or REM (rapid eye movement) sleep. This is when you dream. It's during this stage of sleep (which occurs about ninety minutes after you first fall asleep and recurs every ninety minutes throughout the night) that your blood flow, brain activity, and breathing increases and muscles become fully relaxed and immobilized. Some experts believe this happens so we can't act out our dreams.

If any of these stages are cut short, or if the overall number of cycles is reduced, the body doesn't have time to repair and restore itself. Over time, this repeated sleeplessness wreaks havoc on every aspect of your body, including on your spirit. (Better Sleep, Better Life, 2015; National Sleep Foundation, 2019)

Create a Bedroom Conducive to Sleep

The ancient Chinese art of feng shui or arranging your home for better health, has some helpful ideas on how to design and arrange your sleep space for better slumber. Try these tips. They may work for you.

- Choose the right paint color. Paints with soft, neutral tones, from soft white and spa blue to warm chocolate brown, help you relax better than vibrant, energetic colors like orange, red, or yellow.

- Clean up. Excess stuff, particularly in the bedroom, can contribute to sleeplessness. According to feng shui, clutter in the bedroom and particularly under the bed can make you anxious.

- Skip mirrors in your immediate bedroom. Mirrors, say feng shui practitioners, indicate movement, which creates restless energy and may inhibit restful sleep.

- Be careful where you place chandeliers or ceiling fans. These shouldn't be right above your bed. According to feng shui, it's a threat to you and bad for your health (and sleep) to have anything hanging over your head as you sleep. (Tchi, 2019; Wong, 2019)

- Ditch the TV in your bedroom. I've already discussed how using electronics around bedtime can interfere with sleep, but feng shui believes that a TV set gives off restless energy even when it's not on, which can trigger insomnia. If you have to have a TV in your bedroom, place it in an armoire or cabinet that you can close off when you go to sleep. And try not to watch it for at least one to two hours before bed.

- Have a few plants, but not too many. One is fine, but too many plants, says feng shui, symbolize growth and movement, interfering with the peaceful energy you want in the bedroom. (Tchi, 2018)

- Place a crystal or two in your bedroom. Selenite is a good option for a crystal if you can only have one in your bedroom. This crystal helps to clear away emotional clutter so you can get a good night's sleep. Black tourmaline is another good option. It is grounding and helps absorb and neutral-ize negative energy. Keep it on your bedside table if you're prone to waking up from bad dreams. Rose quartz is always a great option in the bedroom because of the loving, soothing energy that it gives off. Other good options include howlite, which helps absorb anxiety, and turquoise, which is cleans-ing and protective.

When using crystals in the bedroom, it's important not to use overly large crystals (they give off too much energy, which can disrupt sleep) and to never store crystals under your bed. They work better by the head of the bed, particu-larly if it's against a solid wall, which helps support you, or under your pillow, though this may be too much energy for some people.

• Use scents to help calm the body, mind, and spirit. The right essential oils have the power to help you relax. Try them in a candle or a diffuser. Top of the relaxation list is calming lav-ender, but others that can help soothe you at night include neroli, Roman chamomile, clary sage, ylang ylang, berga-mot, sandalwood, and vetiver.

Where Do You Go from Here?

A healthy body, robust spirit, and youthful radiant skin depend so much on your internal state of health and well-being. What you eat, how you manage stress, how you move, how you care for your spiritual self, and how you sleep are all critical components of your health and the state of your skin.

Follow as many of the tips that I include in the previous chap-ters as you can and you're on your way to living a healthier life.

Even if you just change one or two things for now, you'll still notice and feel a difference. When it comes to mindful beauty, the last component is what you do to your skin physically, from the outside. This is what I'm going to address in the next chapter.

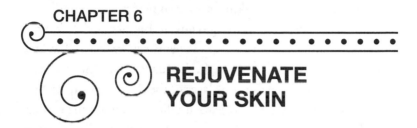

CHAPTER 6

REJUVENATE YOUR SKIN

A HEALTHY BODY, MIND, and spirit creates an inner balance that results in radiant, healthy skin on the outside. This is the reason, as an osteopathic dermatologist, that I've focused on developing your spiritual self, managing stress, eating healthy, exercising, and getting enough sleep *before* discussing how you can better care for your skin on the outside. I know that when you're healthy and feeling good, you have a radiance about you that comes from a body and soul that's nourished. I also know that doing so gives you more confidence in yourself and improves your overall outlook on life.

There's a reason all these healthy living tweaks affect how you look on the outside: the skin is your body's largest organ. Whatever you do to your body affects your skin. Nutrients from whole foods like fruits, vegetables, whole grains, legumes, proteins, and healthy fats help to feed skin cells, build collagen that makes skin look and feel youthful, and protect the skin from the environment around you. Getting regular exercise boosts circulation to the skin, bathing skin cells in a fresh dose of oxygen and nutrients and boosting healthy radiance in the process. And de-stressing and getting enough sleep can regulate levels of hormones in the body, which can calm the body and the skin, helping to prevent skin conditions like acne and psoriasis. Everything is linked. But first, let's talk more about the skin. It covers an average of twenty square feet and weighs about six percent of our total weight. It's made up of three layers.

The epidermis is the topmost layer of the skin that's thickest on the soles of the feet and thinnest around the eyes and on the eyelids. Overall, this layer is extremely thin (only about a tenth of a millimeter in thickness or about the thickness of one sheet of paper) and is the layer of skin that you see. The outermost layer of the epidermis is called the *stratum corneum*. It helps protect the body from the environment and from bacteria, viruses, chemicals, and ultraviolet light. It also traps water in the skin, keeping it hydrated. Without the proper nutrients, the skin's barrier (which is made up of layers of flattened cells) can break down, making it more prone to skin problems like infections, dry skin, and more.

In fact, it's in the epidermis that new skin cells are created. This constant regeneration of cells is one reason it's important to keep this layer exfoliated. Manually removing dry, dead skin cells allows for the healthy, new, radiant cells to showcase themselves. A thickened stratum corneum can feel rough and dry and gives skin a dull appearance.

It's also in the epidermis that melanin, the pigment that gives your skin and hair color, is produced. Melanin is critical to the skin's protection against the sun's ultraviolet rays. When the skin tans, this is melanin in action. It's the body's way of protecting itself.

The dermis is the second layer of skin that gives the skin its flexibility and strength. It's thinnest on the eyelids and thickest on the back (the dermis on the back is about thirty times as thick as the dermis on the eyelids). The dermis produces sweat, helps you feel (as a result of the nerves present in this layer), grows hair, makes sebum or oil thanks to sebaceous glands that secrete sebum into hair follicles, and brings blood to the skin through blood vessels.

It's in the dermis that the structural proteins, collagen and elastin, are found. These proteins are what keep the skin firm and elastic. (When you pull on your skin and it snaps back into place, this is a sign of elasticity.) It's also in the dermis that hyaluronic acid is found. This substance helps the skin hold on to water and stay hydrated. This is also what helps our faces retain youthful fullness.

Lymph vessels are also located in the dermis. These are your body's drainage system and work to cleanse, detox, and maintain proper fluid levels in the skin. They transport lymph fluid throughout the body. It's this lymph fluid that contains white blood cells, which are key to fighting bacteria and viruses. One of the best things you can do to keep your lymph fluid pumping throughout the skin is regular daily movement. Another good way to keep lymph flowing properly and doing its job is through dry brushing. To dry brush, simply take a natural bristled dry brush (available from most bath and beauty stores) and, starting from your feet, firmly but gently brush your skin in circular motions moving in the direction of the heart. Be sure to do your feet, legs, belly, chest, arms, neck, and even your face. It should take about five to ten minutes and can be done in the morning before your shower. You'll notice your skin has a rosier glow afterward. This is an outward sign that you've boosted the circulation and lymph flow in your skin.

The subcutaneous layer (or hypodermis) is the bottommost layer of skin. It's where fat and connective tissue (which connects the skin to the muscles and the bones) is found. It's also where larger blood vessels and nerves are located. It's this layer that controls the temperature of the body.

This layer is thickest on the buttocks and abdomen, providing caloric reserves, insulation, and cushioning. It also gives skin its youthful volume. With age, this layer thins and shifts.

Why Do We Age?

As we get older, all the processes in our body start to slow down. This is dictated by our genes, but it's also affected by the environment around us and our daily habits. In fact, there are two types of aging: intrinsic and extrinsic. Intrinsic (which means "from the inside") aging has to do with your genes or characteristics of aging that you got from your parents, your grandparents, your great-grandparents, and so on down the line.

Many patients talk with me about the genes they inherited from their parents or grandparents. But, in reality, our genes and how we age goes back much further in our lineage. Our genes date back to our ancestors. Though it's hard to know how your ancestors aged, a good place to start is seeing how your mom or dad or grandparents aged, as this will be a starting point to assess how you'll age too. Keep in mind, your lifestyle and habits may be much different from your parents or grandparents, which may make a difference in how you age.

Then there's extrinsic aging (which means "from the outside"). This has everything to do with the environmental factors (like UV light and pollution) that surround you, as well as your diet, your stress levels and how you manage them, how much sleep you get, whether or not you smoke, and what things your skin is exposed to on a daily basis. When discussing healthy habits, it's the extrinsic aging that we've addressed in the first part of this book. In this chapter, we'll be talking about other extrinsic factors, such as sun exposure and the products that you use on your skin.

Antioxidants: Why They Make a Difference

Free radicals are highly destructive molecules in our bodies, including in our skin, that can destroy cells, and over time, trigger diseases like cancer. These molecules are highly destructive because they're missing something called an electron, which is necessary to keep them stable. They're most stable when they're in pairs. When they're not, they attack other cells in an effort to steal an electron and create a pair with their own odd electron. But, in stealing an electron, they leave another molecule without an electron, thereby making it unstable and creating even more destructive free radicals in the process.

Free radicals trigger a process in the body called oxidation. This is just a scientific word to describe what happens when an apple turns brown after you cut it. A similar "browning" process occurs inside our bodies as a result of free radicals. This oxidation, as well as the normal aging process, shortens the telomeres in our cells. As I mentioned earlier, these are the "plastic tips" on the "shoelaces" at each end of our chromosomes or DNA in each of our cells. They protect the end of the chromosome from deteriorating so cells can continue to divide and tissue can regenerate.

Antioxidants provide free radicals with the extra electron they need, stabilizing the free radical, neutralizing it, and rendering it harmless. Antioxidants work because they stop free radicals in their tracks, preventing a cascade of negative effects in the body and on the skin. Simply put, antioxidants are nature's great neutralizers.

With antioxidants being so critical to balance in our body, it makes perfect sense that nature has provided our bodies with their own free-radical-fighting antioxidants like vitamin C, vitamin E, and co-enzyme Q_{10}. These are common supplements today, but the body manufactures its own supply as well. All of these antioxidants are designed to neutralize free radicals that our body is exposed to, but in a modern society with plenty of pollution and pesticides, our bodies' systems can easily get overwhelmed. When this happens, it creates a state of oxidative stress in the body that, over time, can trigger premature aging, of both the body and the skin, and lead to disease.

Eating a diet rich in brightly colored fruits and veggies is one of the best ways to shore up our body's supply of antioxidants. Minerals like selenium, manganese, copper, and zinc, as well as vitamins like A, C, and E, are all antioxidants found in healthy foods. Other sources of antioxidants include coffee beans; green, white, and black tea; and cocoa. (Rhodes et al, 2014; Lobo et al, 2010)

When applied topically, antioxidants help calm redness and decrease skin inflammation. When ingested, antioxidants help protect against damage from the sun's ultraviolet (UV) rays. One study, published in the *British Journal of Nutrition*, found that drinking two cups of green tea every day, along with taking the antioxidant vitamin C, can reduce the effects of the sun's ultraviolet (UV) radiation on the skin. According to the researchers, the antioxidants in green tea make the skin more resilient to the effects of the sun's UV rays, thereby helping to prevent premature aging of the skin and possibly even skin cancer. But this doesn't mean you can drink green tea, along with your vitamin C supplement, and skip the sunscreen. The antioxidants just offer *additional* protection to keep your skin at its healthy, radiant best.

Resveratrol is an antioxidant that can be found in many plants and has been found to protect them from the sun's UV damage and from other environmental stressors. Food sources include grape juice, peanuts, and ripe berries. Resveratrol has also been found to help prevent diseases like type 2 diabetes and cardiovascular disease. What's more, when used topically, resveratrol was shown in one study—published in the *Journal of Cosmetic Dermatology*—to work synergistically with vitamin E to help prevent the domino effect of skin cell changes that result from the natural aging process and exposure to the ultraviolet light and pollution in the environment around us. (Ernst, 2015; Wein, 2019; Farris, 2015)

Other antioxidants that seem to help the skin when applied topically include coffee fruit (the berry of the coffee plant), green tea, vitamin C, vitamin E, coenzyme Q_{10}, and azelaic acid. It's been demonstrated, for example, by Duke University researchers that topical use of antioxidants vitamin C and E can provide additional protection from oxidative damage, slow skin aging, and improve the appearance of the skin. (Quevedo et al, 2000; Lin et al, 2003)

Sun Exposure and Your Skin

Just fifteen minutes of sun exposure can age you. That's what an Australian study found, which is why I advise all my patients to be careful when out in the sun and to apply sun protection whenever they're exposed to the sun's UV rays. It doesn't matter how great your genes are; if you're exposed to the sun, your skin will age faster than normal and you'll have a higher risk of skin cancer. In fact, the sun is responsible for the majority (80 percent) of skin aging, according to research published in the journal *Clinical, Cosmetic, and Investigational Dermatology*. The researchers explained that sun exposure causes hyperpigmentation, reduced skin elasticity, and changes in skin texture—along with fine lines and wrinkles. Plus, the effect of exposure to the sun's ultraviolet rays increases with age. After the age of fifty, people who are exposed to the sun look older than their actual age. (Hughes et al, 2013)

What does this mean for you? Does it mean you should never go out in the sun? No. Knowing what the sun can do to your skin can help you to make better choices, specifically avoiding deliberately trying to get a tan. Most people don't realize that a tan results from injury to the skin's DNA. The skin darkens in an attempt to prevent further DNA damage. Over time, this continued injury to the skin triggers mutations that can lead to skin cancer, the most frequently diagnosed cancer in the United States, with one in five Americans developing it in their lifetime. In fact, the incidence of melanoma (the most dangerous form of skin cancer) is increasing faster than any other cancer.

With all the information circulating about the benefits of vitamin D, many of my patients are telling me that being out in the sun is actually good for them. While exposure to sunlight does help the body make vitamin D, the American Academy of Dermatology doesn't recommend getting your vitamin D from the sun because of the risks of sunlight exposure. Instead, get vitamin D from your diet or a supplement, if necessary. (Sivamani et al, 2009)

Why exactly does the sun trigger so much damage in the skin? One reason is that the sun's ultraviolet (UV) radiation suppresses the immune system, which is why people with herpes break out in cold sores after exposure to the sun. The other reason is that the sun's rays penetrate deep into the skin, triggering damage to the cells and to the skin-firming proteins collagen and elastin. What's more, exposure to UV radiation reduces collagen production in the skin. The sun not only damages the collagen that you have, it also reduces its production. When you understand it like this, you begin to understand why many years of exposure to the sun results in skin that looks older than it actually is. (Hughes et al, 2013)

Understanding the sun's rays, however, and how and why they penetrate the skin, is helpful to understanding how all this damage is done when you're out in the sun. Here's a quick primer:

The sun's ultraviolet or UV rays are divided into UVA rays, UVB rays, and UVC rays. All are invisible to the human eye and all UV radiation can damage the skin's cellular DNA, triggering genetic mutations, which can cause cancer. For years, it was thought that UVB rays were the most damaging to the skin, but it's only been in recent years that scientists have discovered that UVA rays, and even infrared rays, are even more harmful. (Flament et al, 2013)

UVA light or ultraviolet A radiation is not filtered by the earth's ozone layer, meaning as much as 95 percent of UVA reaches the earth's surface. This light penetrates deep in the skin into the mid-dermis and is responsible for tanning and also for skin cancer; eye damage, including cataracts; and the breakdown of collagen, the main structural protein responsible for supporting the skin. What's more, these UV rays are present year-round, at all times of the day, and can penetrate through clouds and glass. A good way to remember what UVA rays do to the skin is the A in UVA is for aging. (Quan et al, 2004)

Tanning beds are particularly bad for your skin because they emit only UVA rays. In fact, tanning beds emit doses of UVA as much as twelve times that of the sun, according to the Skin Cancer Foundation. (Sarnoff, 2011; Peeples, 2010)

UVB light or ultraviolet B radiation is somewhat filtered by the earth's ozone layer, but it only makes up about 4 to 5 percent of UV light (UVA makes up the rest). This UV light does not penetrate as deep as UVA rays. It penetrates to the basal, or bottom, layer of the epidermis, where melanocytes, the cells responsible for pigment, are found. This is the type of light that can cause burning of the skin as well as tanning, skin cancer, and eye damage like cataracts. While UVA rays are present at all times of the day, year-round, UVB radiation is most prevalent between 10 a.m. and 3 p.m. and it doesn't penetrate glass. A good way to remember what UVB rays do to the skin is the B in UVB is for burning.

UVC light or ultraviolet C radiation is completely filtered out by the ozone layer, so zero percent of it reaches the earth's surface.

Infrared light or infrared (IR) radiation can trigger inflammation and is also responsible for changes in the skin that can lead to premature aging. It's divided into IR-A, IR-B, and IR-C radiation, thermal heat, and visible light. New evidence demonstrates that solar aging is a combination of UVA and UVB ultraviolet photo-aging (which constitutes about 6 percent of total solar radiation), visible light aging (which makes up almost 40 percent of total solar radiation), infrared aging (which represents about 54 percent of total solar radiation), and thermal or heat aging. Thermal aging occurs from visible light and infrared radiation.

Free radicals are activated by the different parts of solar radiation and heat. The negative effects of solar light on the skin, in the past, were attributed to wavelengths in the UVA and UVB range. But we now know that IR and visible light can also play a part in extrinsic skin aging as well as skin cancer. Infrared radiation also transmits heat energy, which contributes to premature skin aging, as seen on baker's hands and on the faces of glass blowers.

The issue with infrared light is that current broad-spectrum sunscreens don't protect the skin against it. This is why it's so important to layer an antioxidant under the current sunscreens to help protect against it and to minimize skin inflammation. Antioxidants have been shown to protect skin cells' DNA, mitochondria, proteins, and membranes, and can help defend the skin from radiation that gets through the sunscreen barrier. Topical antioxidants and sunscreens work together synergistically to protect the skin.

To protect yourself from any of the sun's UV rays, consider these tips:

- **Wear a broad-spectrum sunscreen that protects against both UVA and UVB rays** whenever you're outdoors, whether it's seven in the morning or three in the afternoon. And do so, too, whether it's sunny or cloudy, as the sun's rays can penetrate through clouds. You can add extra layers of protection for the skin by applying topical antioxidants under your sunscreen. Antioxidants have been shown to neutralize free radical production and protect the skin from ultraviolet damage. Topical antioxidants and sunscreens work synergistically to protect the skin.

  Ultraviolet rays can also reflect off sand, snow, water, and concrete, so just because you're under an umbrella or covering doesn't mean you don't need sunscreen. And know, too, that if you're in high altitude areas, there's less atmosphere to absorb the harmful ultraviolet rays, so you're getting more radiation, another reason to apply (and reapply) sunscreen.

- **Use enough sunscreen.** You need a golf-ball-size amount of sunscreen (about one ounce or enough to fill a shot glass, though this should be adjusted based on body size) for the entire body every two hours. Most people don't use enough.

- **Do your best to avoid the sun between 10 a.m. and 3 p.m.,** when the sun's UVB rays are most prevalent. And seek shade whenever possible. If you have to be out in the sun during this time, be sure to apply and reapply SPF, wear a hat, and wear sunglasses.

- **Avoid tanning beds.** People who use a tanning bed are 2.5 times more likely to develop a type of skin cancer called squamous cell carcinoma, and 1.5 times more likely to develop a type of skin cancer called basal cell carcinoma. In fact, according to research from the University of Minnesota, when teens use tanning beds, they increase their risk of melanoma (the deadliest kind of skin cancer) by almost 75 percent.

- **Consider adding UV-protective film to your car's side and rear windows** if you drive a lot. Only front windshields typically have it. The sun's UV rays shine through car windows, and research from the *Journal of the American Academy of Dermatology* shows that the left side of the face in US drivers is more aged in appearance and more skin cancer prone than the right side. Being sure to apply sunscreen before driving can help too. (Butler, 2010)

- **Cover up.** Clothing is UV protective. Thicker shirts have more SPF than thinner ones, and darker colors give you more SPF protection than lighter colors. Clothing labeled UPF (ultraviolet protection factor) is also specifically protective against the sun's ultraviolet rays.

- **Wear UV-protective sunglasses** whenever you're outdoors to shield your eyes from the sun's damaging UV rays. Most sunglasses are UV-protective, but to be sure, look for the "100% UV protection" sticker on the lenses.

- **Live a healthy lifestyle.** It's long been known that exposure to the sun's ultraviolet rays has been linked to the skin cancer melanoma. But now German researchers have discovered that lifestyle factors play a role as well. The researchers, at the University of Osnabrück, discovered that something in the skin called MicroRNA's (or MiRs), which are regulators of genes, become overwhelmed from exposure to things like smoking, air pollution, chronic inflammation, chemicals, a high-fat/high-sugar diet, and a sedentary lifestyle. When these MiRs become overwhelmed from this exposure, benign melanocytes (pigment cells) can easily transition into melanoma skin cancer. This is just another reason why a healthy lifestyle is important to not just a healthy body, but to healthy skin too. (Jancin, 2016)

  And just a note about smoking. If you smoke, I know you're already aware of its health risks. But it also affects how you look, which many smokers don't realize. Research from Case Western Reserve University in Ohio has shown that the nicotine in tobacco causes blood vessels in our skin to narrow, limiting the oxygen and nutrients it needs and the removal of waste products it doesn't need. The result: delayed wound healing and the production of free radicals that break down the skin-firming proteins collagen and elastin, as well as DNA. E-cigarettes need to be used with caution too. Nevada-based researchers have found that the vapor from these e-cigarettes still contains chemicals that have similar effects. (Okada, 2013; Rivas, 2013; Science-Daily, 2018)

- **Get enough probiotics.** Another reason to eat them is more youthful looking skin. Research from Japan shows that ingesting probiotics seems to also protect against photo-aging from the sun's ultraviolet B rays. The signs of photo-aging include hyperpigmentation, rough skin, fine lines and wrinkles, and sagging skin. Probiotics seem to work by suppressing water loss from the skin and preventing UVB-triggered changes in the skin like skin thickening and overall damage. You don't necessarily need to take a supplement. You can get probiotics from yogurt and fermented foods like sauerkraut and kefir. (Rupani, 2015; Satoh et al, 2015)

The Visible Signs of Aging

An inverted pyramid (also called the triangle of youth) is often used to represent a youthful face. This includes healthy, full, vibrant cheeks and fullness in the area around the eyes. As we age, the effects of gravity play a role as everything starts to move downward and we become more of an upright pyramid. We lose volume in our upper face from our forehead and cheeks. The eyebrows start to drop and we develop eyelid wrinkles. Fine lines and wrinkles appear around the mouth, too, along with a thinning of the lips. There's also a dimpling of the chin. Some of the visible signs of skin aging include:

- Dull skin appearance due to slower turnover of radiant new skin cells
- Facial expression lines (how wrinkled you become depends largely on how much sun you have been exposed to in your lifetime)
- Telangiectasias or small, superficial blood vessels on the surface of the skin

- Dry, rough skin and uneven texture
- Laxity or sagging
- Irregular brown pigmentation
- Purpura or bruising
- DNA mutations and precancerous and/or cancerous changes in the skin

Your Home Skincare Routine

Many first-time patients come into my office interested in age-erasing cosmetic procedures, but they don't take care of their skin at home. They don't have a dedicated skincare regimen or use sunscreen daily. A simple at-home regimen can do wonders for the skin. This includes cleansing and exfoliating, replenishing the skin with key nutrients/ingredients, protecting it, and moisturizing it. This is the foundation of care that addresses all three layers of the skin. It helps repair damage that's already occurred and prevents future damage.

Keep in mind that it's important to maintain your skin all over, not just on your face, which is the area most people are most concerned about. I often advise my patients not to forget the areas that surround the face—the neck, chest, shoulders, and upper back—as well as the lower legs, arms, and the back of the hands. The skin on the body has a much slower cell turnover rate than the face, so daily maintenance is needed. This is why you should treat all of the areas of the skin with the same maintenance routine and rejuvenation methods. Remember, environmental damage occurs all over the body, though this damage to the face is the most visible.

Here are the key steps that I recommend to all of my patients:

- **Gently cleanse your skin.** Washing your face, morning and night, helps to remove makeup and/or sunscreen, daytime grime that's collected on your face and in your pores, bacteria, dead skin cells, and skin oil. It also preps your skin for any products you're applying afterward, helping them to be better absorbed. Leaving makeup or sunscreen on at night can inhibit the skin's natural exfoliating process.

When you're washing your face or applying any products to the skin, do so gently from the neck upward to the forehead. Applying products in a downward motion tugs down on the skin, which can contribute to sagging over time. Rubbing or tugging at the skin, particularly in the delicate area around the eyes, can also have this effect.

Be sure to always use a gentle cleanser that's free from chemicals like parabens, the antibacterial triclosan, perfumes, and dyes, all of which can irritate sensitive skin. If a cleanser is too harsh, it can strip the skin of natural oils, irritating the skin. And it's also a good idea to use lukewarm, not hot or cold, water. Extreme temperatures strip skin's oils and trigger broken capillaries, the tiny blood vessels on skin's surface. Water that's too hot or too cold can also irritate sensitive and rosacea-prone skin.

You may also need to use a gentle makeup remover before cleansing, particularly around your eyes if you use waterproof makeup. Not properly removing eye makeup is a sure way to trigger eye irritations. One of my favorite makeup removers is coconut oil on a cotton ball. It's gentle enough for all skin types, and effective. When cleansing around the eyes, gently dab (don't rub) the remover. Since the skin around the eyes is the thinnest anywhere on the body, it's easy to rub and tug and damage this delicate skin, triggering fine lines and deeper wrinkles called "crow's feet" around the eyes.

Gently dab (never rub) skin with a towel to dry. Harsh rubbing with a towel or washcloth during the cleansing process can irritate skin and, over time, the trauma can contribute to fine lines and wrinkles.

You may want to finish with a toner, which can help remove any dirt or makeup left behind after cleansing. I'm a big advocate of alcohol-free toners. Alcohol can strip the skin of natural oils, leaving the complexion tight, dry, and in desperate need of moisture. It can also trigger excess oil production, which can aggravate already oily skin. Keep in mind that a toner is not essential to a skincare regimen, but I've found that many of my patients like the clean feeling a toner can give their skin. Some of my patients even like to use it throughout the day to help reduce shine and freshen skin. If you want to try a toner, look for ones that feed the skin with gentle, natural ingredients like witch hazel, green tea, rosemary, grapeseed, and/or chamomile. Toners can also contain exfoliating ingredients like glycolic, salicylic, and/or azelaic acid, which can help slough off dead skin cells, keeping pores clear and the complexion radiant.

• **Exfoliate regularly.** The skin is continually renewing itself, shedding dull, old skin cells to make way for newer, more radiant skin cells. This is a process that takes place in the skin every twenty-eight days, though as we get older this process slows down. This is one reason skin looks duller as you get older, particularly if you don't exfoliate regularly.

The dead skin cells, along with sun exposure, pollution, dirt and grime, makeup, and the skin's oils all work their way into the skin's pores, making these pores look larger and potentially clogging them too. Exfoliating daily gets rid of this debris on the skin, making skin smoother and less likely to break out. Exfoliating has also been shown to help the absorption of the serums, lotions, and/or creams, particularly those containing the antioxidant vitamin C, that you apply to your skin.

When we exfoliate, the cells in the outermost layer of the skin send signals to the layers of cells below to increase new cell production. This speeds up cell renewal and transforms dull skin almost immediately, adding radiance. Exfoliating can also even out skin tone and pigmentation.

There are two ways to exfoliate: manual and chemical. Physical scrubs, electronic cleansing brushes, and even cleansing sponges or washcloths are all ways to physically exfoliate the skin. A word of caution, however: scrubs that contain crushed seeds or nut shells are too rough for the face and may cause microscopic tears, along with resulting irritation and inflammation in your skin. Chemical exfoliation, on the other hand, sounds unnatural, but it's actually not. There are plenty of natural "chemical" exfoliators, in the form of foaming cleansers, home peels, serums, and stronger in-office peels. These work by "ungluing" the dead cells from your skin so they can be washed away.

The most common chemical exfoliators include:

Alpha hydroxy acids (AHAs) are acids found naturally in the sugars of plants or milk. There are five AHAs: citric (from citrus fruits), tartaric (from grapes), malic (from apples), glycolic (from sugar cane), and lactic (from milk). They're all water soluble, which means they can't penetrate the skin's sebum, which is why these acids are not ideal for oily skin or skin prone to breakouts. Like other chemical exfoliators, AHAs can increase sensitivity to the sun, which is why you need to wear SPF daily.

Beta hydroxy acids (BHAs) are essentially salicylic acid, derived from acetylsalicylic acid or aspirin. These differ from alpha hydroxy acids in that they're lipid or oil soluble, meaning they're able to penetrate through sebum into pores, exfoliating and getting rid of the debris that can clog pores and contribute to breakouts.

Beta hydroxy acids have been shown to improve the signs of aging, namely fine lines and wrinkles, rough skin, and hyperpigmentation, after at least six months of daily application. But they can also increase sun sensitivity by 50 percent, which means you have to use daily sun protection when you use beta hydroxy acids. (Brannon, 2019)

Azelaic acid, which is derived from wheat, barley, and rye, is a jack-of-all-trades, so to speak. It exfoliates the skin and it's an antibacterial and anti-inflammatory, making it a good option for acne-prone skin. Not to mention it also prevents hyperpigmentation by regulating the production of melanin. Like beta hydroxy acids, it can make skin sun sensitive, so use a daily sunscreen when using products that contain this chemical exfoliant.

Retinoids vary in strength from prescription-strength— which go by names like tretinoin (a.k.a. Retin-A or Renova) and tazarotene (or Tazorac)—to weaker over-the-counter versions like retinyl palmitate, retinol, and retinaldehyde.

All retinoids are derivatives of vitamin A; these work by sloughing off dead skin cells to prevent pores from clogging, even out skin tone, and help prevent premature aging of the skin. They can also stimulate the production of collagen and hyaluronic acid. These are best used on the skin at night, as retinoids can make the skin extremely sensitive to the sun and they can break down in sunlight, making them less effective. This is why applying daily sun protection when using these products is an absolute must.

When it comes to exfoliating, more is definitely *not* better. Too much exfoliating (i.e., using a manual exfoliator followed by a chemical one, while you're applying retinoids at night) can leave skin irritated. I recommend daily exfoliation to my patients. If this makes skin irritated, then switch to every other day or every third or fourth day. If your skin can tolerate daily exfoliation, then you can work up to twice-daily exfoliation.

- **Replenish the skin with antioxidants.** The skin's natural antioxidants include vitamin C, found naturally in high levels in both the epidermis and the dermis where it's critical to the production of the skin-firming proteins collagen and elastin. But the skin's antioxidants are depleted by daily exposure to the sun's UV rays and to environmental pollution from car exhaust and smoke, including secondhand cigarette smoke.

What can help? A diet rich in antioxidants and topical antioxidants. One study, in the *American Journal of Clinical Nutrition*, found that eating a diet high in vitamin C-rich foods can actually keep your skin healthier and more youthful looking. Topical antioxidants, on the other hand, replenish the skin's stores from the outside in, thereby helping to neutralize the effects of free radical damage. They also fight inflammation and, in many cases, they help the skin stay moisturized. What's more, antioxidants like vitamins C and E have been shown to help prevent UV-induced damage to the skin, keeping the skin youthful looking longer. In doing so, they protect the collagen that you already have and stimulate cells in the skin called fibroblasts (found in the dermis) to produce even more collagen. (Cosgrove et al, 2007: Quevedo et al, 2000)

Placing antioxidants like vitamin C directly on the skin can offer great benefits by directly targeting the desired areas of improvement. This is why I recommend that all my patients apply topical antioxidants and, when used during the day, layer these antioxidants under a sunscreen. Research presented at the World Congress of Dermatology showed that pre-treating the skin with vitamin C *under* a sunscreen prior to going out in the sun or being exposed to pollution seems to prevent significant free radical damage. It's because of studies like this that I recommend layering a concentrated antioxidant product under sunscreen. (Lin et al, 2003; SkinInc., 2015)

When choosing an antioxidant product, look for airless containers that preserve the potency of the antioxidants inside. These containers also keep skincare products free from bacterial, viral, or fungal contamination. Think about what happens to that apple that's been left out on the counter. The same "rusting" happens to the antioxidants in products, so to speak. Oxygen causes antioxidants to lose their potency. Every time you open your jar or bottle of antioxidants, you're exposing the product to air and decreasing its potency. (Duarte et al, 2009)

• **Apply sunscreen.** Sun is the number one cause of premature aging. That's why I recommend to all my patients that they apply SPF (sun protection factor), be it in a sunscreen, a foundation, a bronzer, whatever, every single day, rain or shine. And if you're out in the sun, you need to reapply every two hours, or more frequently if you're in and out of the water, sweating, and/or drying off, which can rub off your protection. Your SPF should offer broad-spectrum protection. This means it protects against both the sun's aging and cancer-causing UVA rays and burning and cancer-causing UVB rays.

Sunscreens are divided into two categories: physical and chemical. Each offers protection from the sun, but does so in a different way.

Chemical sunscreens work by absorbing ultraviolet radiation. Since they're absorbed into the skin, these sunscreens are more commonly associated with skin irritation. The key to the effectiveness of these products, though, is you need to apply them at least thirty minutes before sun exposure to give them time to work. One of the most common chemical sunscreen ingredients is oxybenzone.

Physical sunscreens are my favorite. These include titanium dioxide, zinc oxide, and magnesium oxide. They work by reflecting and scattering the sun's ultraviolet radiation. Look for these ingredients in non-nano formulations that are designed to *not* be absorbed by the skin. Instead, they sit on the skin and act as a physical block and are well tolerated by people of all skin types, including sensitive skin and rosacea-prone skin. They work immediately upon application, so you don't have to wait before being exposed to the sun.

• **Moisturize as needed**. While the skin produces its own oil, called sebum, every skin type still needs to add extra hydration. Frequent skin washing and daily environmental damage can all strip the skin of its natural oils. It's best to apply moisturizer within about three minutes of washing and gently patting your skin dry. This helps keep any water present in the skin from evaporating. Look for moisturizers that add nutrients, such as antioxidants, back into the skin.

I always recommend that my patients use a moisturizer day and night for optimum hydration. When your skin is properly hydrated, it's even-toned and even-textured and fine lines and wrinkles are much less noticeable. Nighttime is especially important, as that's when the body undergoes most of its repair, including repair and rejuvenation of the skin. Skin temperature actually rises at night, which can lead to water loss, another reason why moisturizing at night is key. (Rising skin temperature also allows for key ingredients to better penetrate.)

There are two forms of moisturizers: humectants and emollients. Humectants draw water into the outer layer of the skin from the environment and from the deeper dermal layer. These enhance your skin's ability to hold on to water and make your skin feel soft and smooth. Hyaluronic acid and glycerin are two types of humectants. Emollients provide a protective film on skin to prevent water loss. These can be oil- or water-based. Some types of emollients include natural oils like avocado or safflower oil.

Here's a guide to what moisturizers you should be using for your skin type:

- Normal/combination skin: Use a lighter, water-based moisturizer
- Oily skin: Apply a lighter, water-based or non-comedogenic moisturizer (lotions and gels are lighter than creams). Moisturizers with exfoliating ingredients like salicylic or azelaic acid can help keep skin clear.
- Dry skin: Use an oil-based cream moisturizer, particularly during cold weather months.
- Sensitive skin: Use soothing ingredients that won't irritate skin. Also steer clear of synthetic dyes, synthetic fragrances, and chemicals like phthalates, parabens, and sulfates.
- Mature skin: Use an oil-based moisturizer to help add moisture to the skin and hold on to hydration already in the skin.

And whatever you do, don't forget your feet. A common problem I hear about from patients as they age is thickened or callused yellow skin on the feet. The issue is that most people don't care for their feet like they do their face and the rest of their body. But our feet need attention too. Here's my two-step daily foot solution: after showering, massage the feet with a pumice stone or other foot exfoliator. Then apply a cream or lotion with a chemical exfoliant like glycolic acid. Be sure to rub all over your feet, including around your toes. If you can put on a pair of socks afterward to help the cream absorb, do so. You'll see a difference in your feet almost immediately.

Oils: Good for Your Skin and Your Scalp

Hair is technically dead, but the skin on the scalp is very much alive and needs regular care. The right oils massaged into the scalp before washing can strengthen the scalp and the hair. After applying oils, cover hair with a shower cap or towel and leave on for thirty to forty-five minutes before washing. The following is a guide to the best hair oils.

- **Almond oil** is rich in key nutrients like polyunsaturated and mono fatty acids, as well as vitamins A, B, and E. It's an emollient, which means it softens the hair, giving it a silky, lustrous texture (as well as softening the skin, when rubbed into it and onto the scalp). It can also nourish and strengthen the hair and boost shine.

- **Argan oil** is an oil extracted from the argan tree, which is native to the Mediterranean region. It's high in fatty acids and antioxidants like vitamins A and E, which is why it's been used for thousands of years to make hair silkier, softer, and shinier. It also shows some benefit as a de-frizzer. It's not greasy, which makes it an effective leave-in conditioner.

- **Avocado oil** is packed with nutrients like vitamins A, B, and E, super-hydrating essential fatty acids, protein, and amino acids, which are compounds critical to hair growth and strength. All can help feed the hair follicles. Since avocado oil is a humectant, locking in moisture, it makes an effective deep conditioner. The essential fatty acids also help to add shine.

- **Coconut oil** has been shown to have antibacterial, antifungal, and antiviral properties, thanks to fatty acids called lauric acid and capric acid. It's also rich in antioxidants and nutrients like vitamins E and K. It penetrates deep into the hair shaft, helping to retain moisture, strengthening strands, and keeping hair soft and hydrated.

- **Extra virgin olive oil,** which is chock-full of healthy fats and antioxidants, is an emollient, meaning it can get down deep into the hair shaft, hydrating and adding softness, body, and shine. There's even some evidence that using olive oil as a topical solution on the hair can also help prevent, or at least stem the tide of hair loss by obstructing production of a hormone called DHT (dihydrotestosterone) that's linked to some types of hair loss.

- **Jojoba oil,** which comes from the seeds/nuts of the jojoba plant, is actually a wax, despite its name, that's very close in composition to human skin oil. It's also packed with antioxidant nutrients like vitamin E, zinc, and selenium. Plus, it's an emollient, which makes it an effective moisturizer. Jojoba oil is also good for smoothing strands and adding shine.

Where Do You Go from Here?

Remember that skin is the largest organ of the body. By balancing out what's going on inside the body, you can achieve healthier, more youthful looking skin. I know that patients who put into practice my healthy skin program look and feel at least ten years younger. And know that it's not about being perfect every day. Sure, we all eat chips, cookies, and other processed foods once in a while or sleep in and skip our exercise routine. Don't beat yourself up about it. What matters is that you get right back on track and continue the good habits I talk about in this book. I can't stress enough: the difference you'll feel (more energy, better sleep, more creativity, and more happiness and inner peace) and the difference you'll see firsthand (healthier, younger-looking skin) will be quite dramatic.

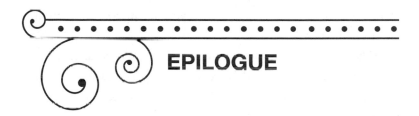

EPILOGUE

YOU ARE AMAZING. You are beautiful. You are unique. You've reached the end of this book's journey and are now ready to continue to move forward on your own path to a healthier, more beautiful you.

Take a look at the lists you put together when you started this book or recount the mental lists you made in your mind. Think about the healthy habits you wanted to incorporate, the spiritual connections you wanted to make, and the lifestyle changes you were eager to put into practice. If you haven't made as many changes as you'd like, remember that inner and outer beauty is a journey, not something that is accomplished just because you finished this book. As I've mentioned throughout the pages of this book, what matters are the small steps you put into practice every single day.

This book should serve as a guide. Refer back to it regularly as you continue to make changes. As Buddha once said: "You must make the effort yourself. The masters only point the way."

What matters are the changes you feel and notice in your own body: how you're less stressed, how you've begun to feel more spiritually connected to your inner self, how you're sleeping, your energy and enthusiasm, how you're getting fewer colds, how you're losing weight without being on a diet, and how your skin glows. By following the tips and advice in this book, you are reinforcing change to your whole person—who you are physically, mentally, emotionally, and spiritually.

When our bodies are truly in a state of healthy balance, it radiates from us in everything that we do. Going back to the ayurvedic concept of the ojas, beauty is truly a reflection of the health of our bodies, our minds, our spirits, and our skin.

May you enjoy true mindful beauty every single day of your life, and may this book continue to be your guide along that journey.

APPENDIX

HEALTHY MEDITERRANEAN RECIPES

Poached Salmon with Lemon Vinaigrette

Salmon is a staple of the Mediterranean diet as it is rich in health- and skin-boosting omega-3 fatty acids and protein.

Ingredients

For the salmon

1 (4-pound) wild salmon fillet, skin off,
    cut into 5-ounce portions

2 celery stalks, diced

2 onions, diced

2 carrots, diced

3 bay leaves

2 cups white wine

8 cups water

For the lemon vinaigrette:

5 garlic cloves, smashed

2 shallots, sliced

2 lemons, zested and juiced

2 cups white wine

Pink Himalayan salt (rich in vital
minerals not found in table salt)

Ground white pepper

2 tablespoons whole-grain mustard

1 cup extra virgin olive oil

2 pounds mesclun greens

1 bunch chives, minced

Directions

For the salmon

Place ingredients in large stockpot and simmer 15 to 20 minutes. Strain stock; season with salt and pepper. In roasting pan, bring stock to a simmer. Submerge salmon in stock; cook to desired doneness (about 20 minutes). Remove salmon with spatula; chill until ready to eat.

For the lemon vinaigrette

Place garlic, shallots, lemon zest, and white wine in pot over medium heat; allow wine to reduce to half. Season with salt, pepper, and juice of lemon. Chill. Add mixture into blender, add mustard. Blend until smooth. Drizzle in olive oil until creamy.

For assembly

Toss greens with lemon vinaigrette. Place poached salmon on salad and drizzle with vinaigrette. Garnish with minced chives.

Portobello Burgers

Portobello mushrooms are a good source of fiber and B vitamins, as well as the antioxidant minerals selenium and potassium. The B vitamins help boost circulation in the body, including in the skin, which can help give you a healthy, radiant glow.

Ingredients

3 Portobello mushrooms

4 tablespoons balsamic vinegar

¼ cup extra virgin olive oil

Pinch of pink Himalayan salt

Pinch of pepper

¼ cup lemon juice

4 garlic cloves, crushed

1 onion, sliced (optional)

Feta cheese (optional)

Directions

Clean mushrooms and remove stems. Combine the next 6 ingredients in a bowl, and marinate the mushrooms in the mixture for three hours. Then grill to desired doneness (about 10 minutes) and top with grilled sliced onion and organic feta cheese.

Black Olive Crusted Haddock

Fish is rich in omega-3 fatty acids, which are good for your body as well as for your skin and hair. You can substitute your favorite fish in place of haddock, if you want. Try to be sure that whatever fish you choose is low in mercury, a neurotoxin that's been linked to a host of health problems including neurological disorders. Other low-mercury seafood includes tilapia, flounder, perch, sole, salmon, sardines, scallops, and shrimp.

Ingredients

1 cup oil-cured pitted black olives
2 cups breadcrumbs
2 cloves garlic
1 shallot
½ bunch parsley
½ bunch chives
Extra virgin olive oil, as needed
Grapeseed oil (for searing)

Directions

Combine olives, breadcrumbs, garlic, shallots, and herbs in a food processor, and pulse until olives are chopped and breadcrumbs are softened. Drizzle in extra olive oil to soften breadcrumbs. Drizzle grapeseed oil (which can be used at very high heat) in the pan, heat pan, then place fish on it and sear just one side. (Searing adds caramelized texture to the outside of the fish, while leaving the inside flaky and tender.) Turn fish over, place in a glass dish and top with olive oil and breadcrumb mixture. Bake in a 350° F oven for 20 minutes.

Three Bean Super Salad

Beans are chock-full of nutrients like protein and fiber and are a perfect replacement in your diet for red meat. This is one of my favorite bean recipes that I make for my family (and one that my grandmother and mother made for me years ago).

Ingredients

15 ounces cannellini (white kidney) beans (cooked)

15 ounces garbanzo beans (cooked)

15 ounces red kidney beans (cooked)

Half an onion, minced

1 clove garlic, minced

2 tablespoons minced fresh parsley

¼ cup extra virgin olive oil

1 lemon, juiced

Salt and black pepper, to taste

1 large tomato, chopped (optional)

Directions

Combine cannellini, garbanzo, and red kidney beans in a mixing bowl. Add onion, garlic, parsley, olive oil, lemon juice, salt, pepper, and tomato. Mix well with a spoon. Serve as a side dish or as a main course over organic mixed greens.

Stuffed Grape Leaves with Kefir Sauce

Grape leaves are a staple of the Mediterranean region and are rich in fiber and vitamins A and K, as well as calcium and iron. These stuffed grape leaves have been passed down from my mother's side of the family. They make a perfect appetizer or main course, when served with a side of vegetables.

Ingredients

1 16-ounce jar grape leaves

1 pound lean ground grass-fed beef*

2 cups rice

2 eggs

½ chopped onion

½ cup extra virgin olive oil

½ cup lemon juice

1 clove garlic, crushed

2 pounds tomatoes, diced

Pinch of pink Himalayan salt

Pinch of ground black pepper

1 tablespoon fresh chopped mint (optional)

1 tablespoon fresh chopped parsley (optional)

If you're going to eat red meat, try to opt for grass-fed red meat as it's been shown to trigger less inflammation in the body.

Directions

Mix together all ingredients except grape leaves. (You can also mix in the fresh chopped mint and/or parsley if you want.) Place mixture inside grape leaves and roll to close. Place on top of each other in a large pot and fill ¾ of the way with water. Add olive oil and lemon juice. Boil over medium heat until tender, and once you've reached desired doneness (about 45 minutes).

Kefir Sauce

This yogurt sauce is rich in good-for-your-gut probiotics (thanks to the healthy bacteria found in yogurt).

Ingredients

1 c. plain kefir whole milk
½ c. cucumber, finely chopped
½ c. fresh dill, finely chopped
2 garlic cloves, minced
1 t. lemon juice
Salt and pepper to taste

Directions

Make the kefir sauce: toss together the kefir, cucumber, dill, garlic, lemon juice, and pinch of salt and pepper. Season to taste, as needed, and set aside. Spoon kefir sauce on top of stuffed grape leaves and serve.

Mediterranean Stuffed Tomatoes

These stuffed tomatoes are packed with antioxidants and vitamin C, all important for healthy, radiant skin and a healthy body.

Ingredients

1 package whole-wheat orzo pasta

1 small handful parsley, chopped

3 ounces feta cheese, crumbled

1 small handful mint leaves, chopped

1 cucumber, diced

¼ cup pine nuts, toasted

2 tablespoons extra virgin olive oil

1 teaspoon lemon juice

6 tomatoes, tops cut off and cored

Salad greens (optional)

You can also add grass-fed ground beef to this if you want.

Directions

Cook pasta, drain, and add the next 7 ingredients to taste. Place inside fresh, whole organic tomatoes and bake at 350°F for 30 minutes. Serve warm, alongside salad greens.

Garlic-y Kale

Kale is an amazing source of nutrients like vitamins A, C, and K and minerals like manganese, copper, and iron. It's great for the skin and the body. This is one of the recipes I frequently make with my family. It's quick and so good for you.

Ingredients

1 bunch kale
2 tablespoons extra virgin olive oil
1 clove garlic, minced
1 small onion, minced (optional)
1 large tomato, chopped (optional)
Salt and pepper, to taste
Red pepper flakes, to taste (optional)

Directions

Remove kale leaves from the stems; rinse under cool water. Heat 2 tablespoons of olive oil and 1 clove minced garlic in a large skillet over medium heat. Once the oil is hot, add the washed kale to the skillet and cover. Stir occasionally, and continue to cook until the kale is wilted. To add variety, add 1 small onion, minced and sautéed and/or 1 large chopped tomato. Don't overcook. Season with salt and pepper and/or red pepper flakes to taste.

Organic Zucchini with Fresh Herbs

Zucchini is chock-full of skin-friendly and health-boosting anti-oxidants like vitamin C, lutein, and zeaxanthin. This is one of my favorite recipes to whip up at home. It's fast and easy and my kids love it!

Ingredients

8 small zucchini (2 pounds)
1 teaspoon pink Himalayan salt
Dash of pepper
¼ cup extra virgin olive oil
2 tablespoons chopped parsley
1 tablespoon snipped chives or dill
1 tablespoon fresh lemon juice

Directions

Wash zucchini and cut into diagonal, ¼-inch thick slices. In a medium skillet bring ½ cup water with salt and pepper to boil. Add zucchini, cook over medium heat, covered, for 10 minutes or until just tender and water has evaporated. Add olive oil, parsley, chives and lemon juice, toss gently to combine. Pour into serving dish; serve warm.

BIBLIOGRAPHY

"A Week's Worth of Camping Synchs Internal Clock to Sunrise and Sunset, CU-Boulder Study Finds." *CU Boulder Today.* University of Colorado: Boulder: August 1, 2013. https://www.colorado.edu/today/2013/08/01/weeks-worth-camping-synchs-internal-clock-sunrise-and-sunset-cu-boulder-study-finds.

Abete, I., D. Parra, and A.B. Crujeiras. "Specific Insulin Sensitivity and Leptin Responses to a Nutritional Treatment of Obesity via a Combination of Energy Restriction and Fatty Fish Intake. " *Journal of Human Nutrition and Dietetics.* September 2008, (21) 6, 591–600. http://www.researchgate.net/publication/23226269_Specific_insulin_sensitivity_and_leptin_responses_to_a_nutritional_treatment_of_obesity_via_a_combination_of_energy_restriction_and_fatty_fish_intake.

Ackerman, Jennifer. "How Bacteria in Our Bodies Protect Our Health." *Scientific American.* 306(6). http://www.scien

tificamerican.com/article/ultimate-social-network-bacte-ria-protects-health/. Accessed March 4, 2019.

"Acupuncture for Chronic Pain." *JAMA Internal Medicine.* October 22, 2012, 72(19), 1444–1453. http://archinte. jamanetwork.com/article.aspx?articleid=1357513.

"Acupuncture for Eczema and Skin Disorders." Pacific College of Oriental Medicine. http://www.pacificcollege.edu/news/ blog/2015/01/16/acupuncture-eczema-skin-disorders. Accessed February 12, 2019.

Adams, Rose, Barb White, and Cynthia Beckett. "The Effects of Massage Therapy on Pain Management in the Acute Care Setting." *International Journal of Therapeutic Massage and Bodywork.* 2010, 3(1), 4–11. http://www.ncbi.nlm.nih. gov/pmc/articles/PMC3091428/.

"Adverse Health Effects of Plastics." *Ecology Center.* http://ecol-ogycenter.org/factsheets/adverse-health-effects-of-plastics/. Accessed March 9, 2019.

Akerstedt, Torbjorn, Johanna Garefelt, Anne Richter, et al. "Work and Sleep—A Prospective Study of Psychosocial Work Factors, Physical Work Factors, and Work Schedul-ing." *Sleep.* 2015, 38(7). https://www.ncbi.nlm.nih.gov/ pubmed/26118559.

"Alzheimer's Linked to Sleeping Pills and Anti-Anxiety Drugs." *Time.* September 10, 2014. http://time.com/3313927/alz-heimers-linked-to-sleeping-pills-and-anti-anxiety-drugs/.

Arab, L. and A. Ang. "A Cross Sectional Study of the Asso-ciation Between Walnut Consumption and Cognitive Function Among Adult U.S. Populations Represented in

NHANES." *The Journal of Nutrition, Health, and Aging.*
March 2015, 19(3), 284–290. http://link.springer.com/
article/10.1007/s12603-014-0569-2#.

Arab, Lenore, and Susan Steck. "Lycopene and Cardiovascular
Disease." *The American Journal of Clinical Nutrition.* June
2000, 71(6): 1691S–1695S. https://academic.oup.com/
ajcn/article/71/6/1691S/4729653.

"Are Telomeres the Key to Aging and Cancer?" *Learn Genetics.*
https://learn.genetics.utah.edu/content/basics/telomeres/.
Accessed February 19, 2019.

Armstrong, Miranda E.G., Jane Green, Gillian K. Reeves, et al.
"Frequent Physical Activity May Not Reduce Vascular Disease Risk as Much as Moderate Activity: Large Prospective
Study of UK Women." *Circulation.* February 2015, 131,
721–729. 10.1161/CIRCULATIONAHA.114.010296.

"Association Between Objectively-Measured Physical Activity and Sleep, NHANES 2005–2006." *Mental Health
and Physical Activity.* December 2011, 4(2): 65–69.
https://www.sciencedirect.com/science/article/abs/pii/
S1755296611000317.

Bae, Sanghyuk, and Yun-Chui Hong. "Exposure to Bisphenol A from Drinking Canned Beverage Increases Blood
Pressure: Randomized Crossover Trial." *Hypertension.*
December 8, 2014. http://hyper.ahajournals.org/content/
early/2014/12/08/HYPERTENSIONAHA.114.04261.
abstract.

Baer, Adam. "The Most Powerful Food Combinations."
Men's Health. https://www.menshealth.com/nutrition/

a19536746/powerful-food-combinations/. Accessed March 3, 2019.

Barbour, Sharon. "Cancer Boost from Whole Carrots." *BBC News.* June 16, 2009. http://news.bbc.co.uk/2/hi/health/8101403.stm.

Barrett, Diane M., PhD. "Maximizing the Nutritional Value of Fruits and Vegetables." University of California: Davis. http://ucce.ucdavis.edu/files/datastore/234-780.pdf. Accessed March 3, 2019.

Barros, Rodrigo. "The Role of the Skin Microbiome in Health and Disease." *MD Magazine.* February 22, 2015. http://www.hcplive.com/conferences/aaaai-2015/The-Role-of-the-Skin-Microbiome-in-Health-and-Disease.

Barry, Susan R., PhD. "How to Grow New Neurons in Your Brain." *Psychology Today.* January 16, 2011. https://www.psychologytoday.com/blog/eyes-the-brain/201101/how-grow-new-neurons-in-your-brain.

"Benzodiazepine Use and Risk of Alzheimer's Disease: Case-Control Study." *BMJ.* 2014: 349. https://www.bmj.com/content/349/bmj.g5205.

Bergland, Christopher. "How Does Yoga Relieve Chronic Pain?" *Psychology Today.* May 27, 2015. https://www.psychologytoday.com/us/blog/the-athletes-way/201505/how-does-yoga-relieve-chronic-pain.

Bhan, Arunoday, Imran Hussain, Kairul I. Ansari, et al. "Bisphenol-A and Diethylstilbestrol Exposure Induces the Expression of Breast Cancer Associated Long Noncoding RNA HOTAIR *in vitro* and *in vivo.*" *The Journal of Ste-*

roid *Biochemistry and Molecular Biology*. May 2014, (141): 160–170. http://www.sciencedirect.com/science/article/pii/S0960076014000314

"Bisphenol A (BPA)." National Institutes of Health, National Institute of Environmental Health Sciences. http://www.niehs.nih.gov/health/topics/agents/sya-bpa/. Accessed March 4, 2019.

Blaylock, Russell, MD. "Stress Depletes Vitamin C." *Newsmax Health*. January 7, 2015. https://www.newsmax.com/health/dr-blaylock/vitamin-c-trauma-cancer-antioxidant/2016/06/22/id/735156/.

Bonwick, Graham, and Catherine S. Birch. "Antioxidants in Fresh and Frozen Fruit and Vegetables: Impact Study of Varying Storage Conditions." University of Chester. http://bfff.co.uk/wp-content/uploads/2013/09/Leatherhead-Chester-Antioxidant-Reports-2013.pdf. Accessed March 3, 2019.

Bowe, Whitney, Nayan Patel, and Alan C. Logan. "Acne Vulgaris: The Role of Oxidative Stress and the Potential Therapeutic Value of Local and Systemic Antioxidants." *Journal of Drugs in Dermatology*. June 2012, 11(6), 742–746. http://www.biomedsearch.com/nih/Acne-vulgaris-role-oxidative-stress/22648222.html.

Brannon, Heather, MD. "Beta Hydroxy Acid." *Verywellhealth.com*. http://dermatology.about.com/cs/skincareproducts/a/bha.htm. Accessed March 18, 2019.

Branson, Ken. "Olive Oil Kills Cancer in Minutes." *Futurity*. February 19, 2015. http://www.futurity.org/olive-oil-cancer-859862/

"Breast Cancer Risk Seems More Affected by Total Body Fat Than Abdominal Fat." BreastCancer. https://www.breast cancer.org/research-news/total-body-fat-affects-risk-more -than-belly-fat. Accessed March 11, 2019.

Broughton, Susan J., Matthew D. W. Piper, Tomoatsu Ikeya, et al. "Longer Lifespan, Altered Metabolism, and Stress Resistance in *Drosophila* from Ablation of Cells Making Insulin-Like Ligands." *PNAS: Proceedings of the National Academy of Sciences.* February 2005, 102(8), 3105–3110. https://www.pnas.org/content/102/8/3105.

Brummit, Jason. "The Role of Massage in Sports Performance and Rehabilitation: Current Evidence and Future Direction." *North American Journal of Sports Physical Therapy.* February 2008, 3(1), 7–21. http://www.ncbi.nlm.nih.gov/pmc/articles/PMC2953308/.

"Brush on The Marinade, Hold Off The Cancerous Compounds." ScienceDaily. June 28, 2007. http://www.science daily.com/releases/2007/06/070627124111.htm.

Buckland, G., A. Agudo, and L. Luján. "Adherence to a Mediterranean Diet and Risk of Gastric Adenocarcinoma Within the European Prospective Investigation into Cancer and Nutrition (EPIC) Cohort Study." *American Journal of Clinical Nutrition.* February 2010, 91(2), 3810–90; http://www.ncbi.nlm.nih.gov/pubmed/20007304.

Buettner, Dan. "The Island Where People Forget to Die." *The New York Times.* October 24, 2012. http://www.nytimes.com/2012/10/28/magazine/the-island-where-people-for get-to-die.html?pagewanted=all&_r=0.

Burton, Neel. "Man's Search for Meaning." *Psychology Today.* May 24, 2012. https://www.psychologytoday.com/us/blog/hide-and-seek/201205/mans-search-meaning.

Butler, S.T. and S.W. Fosko. "Increase Prevalence of Left-Sided Skin Cancers." *Journal of the American Academy of Dermatology.* December 2010, 63(6): 1006–10. https://www.ncbi.nlm.nih.gov/pubmed/20226568.

Cabrera, C., R. Artacho, and R. Gimenez, "Beneficial Effects of Green Tea—A Review." *Journal of the American College of Nutrition.* April 2006, 25(2): 79–99. https://www.ncbi.nlm.nih.gov/pubmed/16582024.

Caldwell, Emily. "Study: Massaging Muscles Facilitates Recovery After Exercise." *The Ohio State University Research News.* August 12, 2008. https://news.osu.edu/study—massaging-muscles-facilitates-recovery-after-exercise/.

Carter, Claire. "Sex is the Secret to Looking Younger, Claims Researcher." *The Telegraph.* July 5, 2013. http://www.telegraph.co.uk/lifestyle/10161279/Sex-is-the-secret-to-looking-younger-claims-researcher.html.

Cavet, M.E., K.L. Harrington, T.R. Vollmer, et al. "Anti-inflammatory and Anti-oxidative Effects of the Green Tea Polyphenol Epigallocatechin Gallate in Human Corneal Epithelial Cells." *Molecular Vision.* February 18, 2011, 17: 533–42. https://www.ncbi.nlm.nih.gov/pubmed/21364905.

"CDC: 9 Million Americans Use Prescription Sleeping Pills." *DailyNews.* August 30, 2013. http://www.nydailynews.

com/life-style/health/cdc-9-million-americans-sleep-ing-pills-article-1.1441778.

Cedernaes, J., F.H. Rangtell, E.K. Axelsson, et al. "Short Sleep Makes Declarative Memories Vulnerable to Stress in Humans." *Sleep.* June 22, 2015. http://www.ncbi.nlm.nih.gov/pubmed/26158890.

Chassaing, Benoit, Ruth E. Ley, and Andrew T. Getwirtz. "Intestinal Epithelial Cell Toll-like Receptor 5 Regulates the Intestinal Microbiota to Prevent Low-Grade Inflammation and Metabolic Syndrome in Mice." *Gastroenterology.* 2014, 147(6), 1363. https://www.ncbi.nlm.nih.gov/pubmed/25172014.

Cho, E., D. Spiegelman, and D.J. Hunter. "Premenopausal Fat Intake and Risk of Breast Cancer." *Journal of the National Cancer Institute.* 95(14): 1079–85; http://www.ncbi.nlm.nih.gov/pubmed/12865454.

Cho, Y.A., J. Kim, A. Shin, et al. "Dietary Patterns and Breast Cancer Risk in Korean Women." *Nutrition and Cancer.* 2010; 62(8): 1161–9. https://www.ncbi.nlm.nih.gov/pubmed/21058205.

"Circadian Rhythms Regulate Skin Stem Cell Metabolism and Expansion, Study Finds." ScienceDaily. January 6, 2015. http://www.sciencedaily.com/releases/2015/01/150106154607.html.

Clay, Rebecca A. "Green is Good for You." *Monitor on Psychology.* April 2001, 32(4), 40. http://www.apa.org/monitor/apr01/greengood.aspx.

Cohen, Sheldon, Denise Janicki-Deverts, Ronald B. Turner, et al. "Does Hugging Provide Stress-Buffering Social Support? A Study of Susceptibility to Upper Respiratory Infection and Illness." *Psychological Science.* December 19, 2014. http://pss.sagepub.com/content/early/2014/12/17/095679 7614559284.

Collingwood, Jane. "Study Probes How Emotions Affect the Immune System." PsychCentral. May 22, 2014. http://psychcentral.com/news/2014/05/22/study-probes-how-emotions-affect-immune-system/70192.html.

Colton, H.R. and B.M. Altevogt. *Sleep Disorders and Sleep Deprivation: An Unmet Public Health Problem.* National Academies Press: Washington, DC, 2006. https://www.ncbi.nlm.nih.gov/books/NBK19961/.

Conley, Mikaela. "Coffee May Reduce the Risk of Heart Failure." ABC News. June 26, 2012. http://abcnews.go.com/Health/coffee-reduce-heart-failure-risk/story?id=16652479.

"Cortisol Decreases and Serotonin and Dopamine Increase Following Massage Therapy." *The International Journal of Neuroscience.* October 2005, 115(10): 1397–413. https://www.ncbi.nlm.nih.gov/pubmed/16162447.

Cosgrove, Maeve C., Oscar H. Franco, Stewart P. Granger, et al. "Dietary Nutrient Intakes and Skin Aging Appearance Among Middle-Aged Women." *The American Journal of Clinical Nutrition.* October 2007, 86(4), 1225–1231. http://ajcn.nutrition.org/content/86/4/1225.

Cottet, V., M. Touvier, A. Fournier, et al. "Postmenopausal Breast Cancer Risk and Dietary Patterns in the E3N-EPIC

Prospective Cohort Study." *American Journal of Epidemiology*. Nov. 15, 2009, 170(10), 1257–67. http://www.ncbi. nlm.nih.gov/pubmed/19828509.

Covas, M.I. "Olive Oil and the Cardiovascular System." *Pharmacology Research*. March 2007, 55 (3), 175–86. http:// www.ncbi.nlm.nih.gov/pubmed/17321749.

Crooks, Valerie C. DSW; James Lubben, DSW, MPH; Diana B. Petitti, MD, MPH; et al. "Social Network, Cognitive Function, and Dementia Incidence Among Elderly Women." *American Journal of Public Health*. July 2008, Volume 98(7), 1221–1227. http://ajph.aphapublications. org/doi/abs/10.2105/AJPH.2007.115923.

Crow, Edith Meszaros, Emilien Jeannot, and Alison Trewhela. "Effectiveness of Iyengar Yoga in Treating Spinal (Back and Neck) Pain: A Systematic Review." *International Journal of Yoga*. January–June 2015, 8(1): 3–14. https://www.ncbi. nlm.nih.gov/pmc/articles/PMC4278133/.

De la Iglesia, Horacio O., Eduardo Fernandez-Duque, Diego A. Golombek, et al. "Access to Electric Light Is Associated with Shorter Sleep Duration in a Traditionally Hunter-Gatherer Community." *Journal of Biological Rhythms*. August 2015, 30(4), 342–350. http://jbr.sagepub.com/ content/30/4/342.

De Lorgeril, M., P. Salen, JL Martin, et al. "Mediterranean Dietary Pattern in a Randomized Trial: Prolonged Survival and Possible Reduced Cancer Rate." *Archives of Internal Medicine*. 1998, 158; 1181–7. http://www.researchgate. net/publication/13659917_Mediterranean_dietary_pat tern_in_a_randomized_trial_prolonged_survival_and_pos sible_reduced_cancer_rate.

"Defective Telomeres Are Now Being Linked to Dozens of Diseases, Including Many Types of Cancer." EurekAlert. July 15, 2015. https://www.eurekalert.org/pub_releases/2015-07/cndi-dta071515.php.

Dennison, H.J., C. Cooper, A.A. Sayer, et al. "Prevention and Optimal Management of Sarcopenia: a Review of Combined Exercise and Nutrition Interventions to Improve Muscle Outcomes in Older People." *Clinical Interventions in Aging.* May 2015, 10, 859–869. http://www.dovepress. com/prevention-and-optimal-management-of-sarcope nia-a-review-of-combined-e-peer-reviewed-article-CIA.

Dewanto, Veronica, Xianzhong Wu, Kafui K. Adom, and Rui Hai Liu. "Thermal Processing Enhances the Nutritional Value of Tomatoes by Increasing Total Antioxidant Activity." *Journal of Agricultural and Food Chemistry.* 2002, 50(10): 3010–3014. http://pubs.acs.org/doi/abs/10.1021/ jf0115589, http://www.news.cornell.edu/stories/2002/04/ cooking-tomatoes-boosts-disease-fighting-power.

Dimitrov, Stoyan, Elaine Hulteng, and Suzi Hong. "Inflammation and Exercise: Inhibition of Monocytic Intracellular TNF Production by Acute Exercise Via β_2-Adrenergic Activation." *Brain, Behavior, and Immunity.* March 2017, 61: 60–68. https://www.sciencedirect.com/science/article/pii/ S0889159116305645.

"Diversifying Your Diet May Make Your Gut Healthier." ScienceDaily. July 14, 2015. http://www.sciencedaily.com/ releases/2015/07/150714142231.html.

"Do Coffee Drinkers Live Longer?" MPR. November 17, 2015. http://www.empr.com/medical-news/reduced -mortality-risk-seen-for-coffee-drinkers/article/454508. Accessed March 4, 2019.

Dolezal, Brett A., Eric V. Neufeld, David M. Boland, et al. "Interrelationship between Sleep and Exercise: A Systematic Review." *Advances in Preventive Medicine.* 2017, 2017: 1364387. https://www.ncbi.nlm.nih.gov/pmc/articles/ PMC5385214/.

Douillard, John. *The 3-Season Diet: Eat the Way Nature Intended.* New York, NY: Harmony, 2001.

"Drinking Up to Five Cups of Coffee a Day May Benefit the Arteries." Medical News Today. March 3, 2015. http:// www.medicalnewstoday.com/articles/290201.php.

"Driving is Linked to More Skin Cancers on the Left Side of the Body." SkinCancer. https://www.skincancer.org/publica tions/sun-and-skin-news/summer-2010-27-2/driving-linked.

Duarte, T.L., M.S. Cooke, and G.D. Jones. "Gene Expression Profiling Reveals New Protective Roles for Vitamin C in Human Skin Cells." *Free Radical Biology and Medicine.* 2009, 46, 78–87. http://www.ncbi.nlm.nih.gov/ pubmed/18973801.

Duraimani, Shanthi, Robert H. Schneider, Otelio S. Randall, et al. "Effects of Lifestyle Modification on Telomerase Gene Expression in Hypertensive Patients: A Pilot Trial of Stress Reduction and Health Education Programs in African Americans." *PLOS One.* November 16, 2015. https://

journals.plos.org/plosone/article%3Fid=10.1371/journal. pone.0142689.

"Eating Grilled Meat 'Increases Risk of Alzheimer's and Diabetes.'" Medical News Today. February 25, 2014. http:// www.medicalnewstoday.com/articles/273155.php.

"Electronic Cigarettes and Emissions: New Chemicals Found Add to Potential Health Risks." *Tobacco-Related Disease Research Program.* http://www.trdrp.org/news/electronic -cigarettes-emissions.html. Accessed March 11, 2019.

Ernst, Diana. "New Evidence on How Certain Foods Provide Protective Health Benefits." MPR. April 13, 2015; http:// www.empr.com/news/new-evidence-on-how-certain-foods -provide-protective-health-benefits/article/408654.

Eskelinen, M.H. and M. Kivipelto. "Caffeine as a Protective Factor in Dementia and Alzheimer's Disease." *Journal of Alzheimer's Disease.* 2010, 20 Supplement 1, S167–74. http://www.ncbi.nlm.nih.gov/pubmed/20182054.

Esser, D., M. Mars, E. Oosterink, et al. "Dark Chocolate Consumption Improves Leukocyte Adhesion Factors and Vascular Function in Overweight Men." *The FASEB Journal.* 2013; 28 (3): 1464–1473. http://www.fasebj.org/content /28/3/1464.

"Estrogen and Breast Cancer Risk: Factors of Exposure." Cornell University Program on Breast Cancer and Environmental Risk Factors. July 2002. http://envirocancer.cornell. edu/factsheet/general/fs10.estrogen.cfm.

Evans, Julie A. and Elizabeth J. Johnson. "The Role of Phytonutrients in Skin Health." *Nutrients.* August 2010, 2(8),

903–28. http://www.ncbi.nlm.nih.gov/pmc/articles/ PMC3257702/.

Evatt, Marian L. "Vitamin D Associations and Sleep Physiology." *Sleep.* 38(2); https://www.ncbi.nlm.nih.gov/pmc/ articles/PMC4288595/. Accessed March 11, 2019.

Farris, Patricia K. "Resveratrol, the Longevity Molecule." Dermatology Times. April 30, 2015. http://dermatologytimes. modernmedicine.com/dermatology-times/news/resver atrol-longevity-molecule?page=0,0.

Ferrante, G., M. Simoni, F. Cibella, et al. "Third-hand Smoke Exposure and Health Hazards in Children." *Monaldi Archives for Chest Disease.* March 2013, 79(1), 38–43. http://www.ncbi.nlm.nih.gov/pubmed/23741945.

Fielding, J.M., K.G. Rowley, P. Cooper, et al. "Increases in Plasma Lycopene Concentration After Consumption of Tomatoes Cooked with Olive Oil." *Asia Pacific Journal of Clinical Nutrition.* 2005, 14(2): 131–36. https://www.ncbi. nlm.nih.gov/pubmed/15927929.

Filomeno, M., C. Bosetti, E. Bodoli, et al. "Mediterranean Diet and Risk of Endometrial Cancer: A Pooled Analysis of Three Italian Case-Control Studies." *British Journal of Cancer.* May 26, 2015, 112, 1816–1821. http://www.nature. com/bjc/journal/v112/n11/full/bjc2015153a.html.

"Five Stages of Sleep." *Better Sleep, Better Life.* June 21, 2015. http://www.better-sleep-better-life.com/five-stages-of-sleep. html.

Flament, Frederic, Roland Bazin, Sabine Laquieze, et al. "Effect of the Sun on Visible Clinical Signs of Aging in

Caucasian Skin." *Clinical, Cosmetic and Investigational Dermatology.* 2013, 6, 221–232. http://www.ncbi.nlm.nih.gov/pmc/articles/PMC3790843/.

Fowler, S.P., K. Williams, and H.P. Hazuda. "Diet soda intake is associated with long-term increases in waist circumference in a biethniccohort of older adults: The San Antonio Longitudinal Study of Aging." *Journal of the American Geriatrics Society.* April 2015, 63(4): 708–15. https://www.ncbi.nlm.nih.gov/pubmed/?term=%E2%80%A2%09Diet+soda+intake+is+associated+with+long-term+increases+in+waist+circumference+in+a+biethnic+cohort+of+older+adults%3A+the+San+Antonio+Longitudinal+Study+of+Aging.

Frankl, Viktor. *Man's Search for Meaning.* New York, NY: Beacon Press, 2006.

"Freezing Blueberries Improves Antioxidant Availability." Newswise. July 22, 2014. http://www.newswise.com/articles/freezing-blueberries-improves-antioxidant-availability.

"Fried and Grilled Meat May Raise Risk of Diabetes and Dementia." *The Guardian.* February 25, 2014. https://www.theguardian.com/science/2014/feb/25/fried-grilled-meat-risk-diabetes-dementia-glycotoxins.

"Fruit and Vegetable Peel Perks." *University of California Berkeley Wellness.* http://www.berkeleywellness.com/healthy-eating/nutrition/slideshow/fruit-vegetable-peel-perks. Accessed March 3, 2019.

G., Shoba, Joy D., Joseph T., et al. "Influence of Piperine on the Pharmacokinetics of Curcumin in Animals and Human

Volunteers." *Planta Medica.* May 1998, 64(4): 353–6. https://www.ncbi.nlm.nih.gov/pubmed/9619120.

Galatzer-Levy, Jeanne. "Massage Therapy Improves Circulation, Eases Muscle Soreness." University of Illinois at Chicago News Center. April 15, 2014. http://news.uic.edu/massage-therapy-improves-circulation-alleviates-muscle-soreness.

Galland, Leo, MD. "Diet and Inflammation." *Nutrition in Clinical Practice.* December 2010, vol. 25, no. 6; 634–40. http://ncp.sagepub.com/content/25/6/634.full.pdf+html.

Gardner, Jane. "Glancing at a Grassy Green Roof Significantly Boosts Concentration." *Medical Xpress.* May 25, 2015. https://medicalxpress.com/news/2015-05-glancing-grassy-green-roof-significantly.html.

Garfinkle, M.S., A. Singhal, W.A. Katz, et al. "Yoga-Based Intervention for Carpal Tunnel Syndrome: A Randomized Trial." *JAMA.* November 11, 1998, 280(18), 1601–3. http://www.ncbi.nlm.nih.gov/pubmed/9820263.

Giugliano, D., A. Ceriello, and K. Esposito. "The Effect of Diet on Inflammation: Emphasis on the Metabolic Syndrome." *Journal of the American College of Cardiology.* Aug. 15, 2006; 48(4): 677–85. http://www.ncbi.nlm.nih.gov/pubmed/16904534?dopt=Citation.

Godman, Heidi. "Regular Exercise Changes the Brain to Improve Memory, Thinking Skills." *Harvard Health Publications.* April 9, 2014. http://www.health.harvard.edu/blog/regular-exercise-changes-brain-improve-memory-thinking-skills-201404097110.

"Good for the Mind, but How About the Body?" *Harvard Health Letter.* September 2008. https://www.health.ha rvard.edu/newsletter_article/Good_for_the_mind_but_ how_about_the_body.

Goodman, Brenda. "Study Links Coffee to Lower Liver Cancer Risk." *HealthDay.* April 9, 2014. http://consumer. healthday.com/vitamins-and-nutrition-information-27/ caffeine-health-news-89/more-java-please-686666.html.

Goodrich, Julia K., Jillian L. Waters, Angela C. Poole, et al. "Human Genetics Shape the Gut Microbiome." *Cell.* November 6, 2014, 159(4), 789–799. http://www.cell. com/cell/abstract/S0092-8674(14)01241-0.

Grindler, Natalia M., Jennifer E. Allsworth, George A. Macones, et al. "Persistent Organic Pollutants and Early Menopause in U.S. Women." *PLOS One.* January 28, 2015. http://journals.plos.org/plosone/article?id=10.1371/ journal.pone.0116057.

Haelle, Tara. "Poor Quality Sleep May Be Linked to a Shrinking Brain." *HealthDay.* September 3, 2014. http:// consumer.healthday.com/senior-citizen-information-31/ misc-aging-news-10/poor-quality-sleep-may-be-linked-to- shrinking-brain-691359.html.

Hagins, Marshall, Wendy Moore, and Andrew Rundle. "Does Practicing Hatha Yoga Satisfy Recommendations for Intensity of Physical Activity Which Improves and Maintains Health and Cardiovascular Fitness?" *BMC Complementary and Alternative Medicine.* 2007. http://www.biomed central.com/1472-6882/7/40.

Halliwell, Barry. "Dietary Polyphenols: Good, Bad, or Indifferent for your Health?" *Cardiovascular Research*. 2007, 73: 341–347. https://www.ncbi.nlm.nih.gov/pubmed/17141749.

"Harms of Cigarette Smoking and Health Benefits of Quitting." *National Cancer Institute*. https://www.cancer.gov/about-cancer/causes-prevention/risk/tobacco/cessation-fact-sheet. Accessed February 12, 2019.

Hartfiel, Ned, Jon Havenhand, Sat Bir Khalsa, et al. "The Effectiveness of Yoga for the Improvement of Well-Being and Resilience to Stress in the Workplace." *Scandinavian Journal of Work, Environment, and Health*. 2011. http://science.naturalnews.com/2011/835887_The_effectiveness_of_yoga_for_the_improvement_of_well_being.html.

"Health Effects of Secondhand Smoke." Centers for Disease Control and Prevention. http://www.cdc.gov/tobacco/data_statistics/fact_sheets/secondhand_smoke/health_effects/. Accessed February 12, 2019.

"Healthy Sleep Duration Linked to Less Sick Time From Work." ScienceDaily. September 3, 2014. http://www.sciencedaily.com/releases/2014/09/140903163633.html.

Healy, Melissa. "When Obesity is an Inherited Trait, Maybe Gut Bacteria is the Link." *LA Times*. November 6, 2014. http://www.latimes.com/science/sciencenow/la-sci-sn-obesity-genes-gut-bacteria-20141106-story.html.

Heid, Markham. "You Asked: Is Sleeping in a Cold Room Better for You?" *Time*. November 26, 2014. http://time.com/3602415/sleep-problems-room-temperature/.

Heinrich, Ulrike, Karin Neukam, Hagen Tronnier, et al. "Long-Term Ingestion of High Flavanol Cocoa Provides Photoprotection against UV-Induced Erythema and Improves Skin Condition in Women." *The Journal of Nutrition.* June 2006, 136(6), 1565–1569. http://jn.nutrition.org/content/136/6/1565.full.

Hellmich, Nanci. "How Sleep Loss Leads to Significant Weight Gain." *USA Today.* July 20, 2014. http://www.usatoday.com/story/news/nation/2014/07/20/sleep-loss-weight-gain/7507503/.

Hensrud, Donald. "Is Too Little Sleep a Cause of Weight Gain?" MayoClinic. http://www.mayoclinic.org/healthy-lifestyle/adult-health/expert-answers/sleep-and-weight-gain/faq-20058198. Accessed March 11, 2019.

Ho, Won Jin, Michael S. Simon, Vedat O. Yildiz, et al. "Antioxidant Micronutrients and the Risk of Renal Cell Carcinoma in the Women's Health Initiative Cohort." *Cancer.* October 9, 2014. http://onlinelibrary.wiley.com/doi/10.1002/cncr.29091/abstract.

Holzman, David C. "What's in a Color? The Unique Human Health Effects of Blue Light." *Environmental Health Perspectives.* Jan. 2010, 118(1), A22–27. http://www.ncbi.nlm.nih.gov/pmc/articles/PMC2831986/.

"Hot Pepper Compound Could Help Hearts." *American Chemical Society.* March 27, 2012. http://www.acs.org/content/acs/en/pressroom/newsreleases/2012/march/hot-pepper-compound-could-help-hearts.html.

"How Does Exercise Help Those With Chronic Insomnia." National Sleep Foundation. https://www.sleepfoundation. org/articles/how-does-exercise-help-those-chronic-insom nia. Accessed March 11, 2019.

"How Does Stress Affect Us?" American Psychological Associ- ation. October 8, 2018. https://psychcentral.com/lib/how- does-stress-affect-us/

Hu, F.B., and W.C. Willett. "Optimal Diets for Prevention of Coronary Heart Disease." *Journal of the American Medical Association.* 2002, 288, 2569–78.

Hughes, M.C.B., G.M. Williams, P. Baker, et al., "Sunscreen and Prevention of Aging." *Annals of Internal Medicine.* June 4, 2013, 158: 781–90. http://annals.org/article.aspx?arti cleid=1691732.

"Impaired Sleep Linked to Lower Pain Tolerance." News- wise. April 30, 2015. http://www.newswise.com/articles/ view/633488/?sc=mwhn.

"Insomnia Associated with Increased Risk of Heart Attack and Stroke." ScienceDaily. https://www.sciencedaily.com/ releases/2017/03/170331120337.htm. Accessed March 11, 2019.

Ishii, Y., S. Sugimoto, N. Izawa, et al. "Oral Administra- tion of Bifidobacterium Breve Attenuates UV-Induced Barrier Perturbation and Oxidative Stress in Hairless Mice Skin." *Archives of Dermatological Research.* July 2014, 306(5): 467–73. https://www.ncbi.nlm.nih.gov/ pubmed/24414333.

Jancin, Bruce. "EADV: Focus on Non-UV Triggers of Melanoma Risk Exposure." *Dermatology News*. December 11, 2016. http://www.edermatologynews.com/specialty-focus/skin-cancers-and-neoplasms/single-article-page/eadv-focus-on-non-uv-triggers-of-melanoma/67080c043b52aad7800cb5e6c4f085be.html.

Jobling, S., T. Reynolds, R. White, et al. "A Variety of Environmentally Persistent Chemicals, including Some Phthalate Plasticizers, are Weakly Estrogenic." *Environmental Health Perspectives*. June 1995, 103(6): 582–587. http://www.ncbi.nlm.nih.gov/pmc/articles/PMC1519124/.

Johnson, Kate. "Probiotic 'Promising' to Prevent and Treat Atopic Dermatitis." *Medscape Multispecialty Medical News*. November 9, 2014. https://www.medscape.com/viewarticle/834650.

Jordan, Rob. "Stanford Researchers Find Mental Health Prescription: Nature." *Stanford News*. June 30, 2015. http://news.stanford.edu/news/2015/june/hiking-mental-health-063015.html.

Kavey, Neil B., M.D. "Why Do We Need Sleep So Much?" NBCNews. http://www.nbcnews.com/id/3076707/ns/technology_and_science-science/t/why-do-we-need-so-much-sleep/. Accessed September 27, 2019.

Keller, E., and V.M. Bzdek. "Effects of Therapeutic Touch on Tension Headache Pain." *Nursing Research*. March-April 1986, 35(2): 101–6. https://www.ncbi.nlm.nih.gov/pubmed/3633503.

Keller, Karsten, and Martin Engelhardt. "Strength and Muscle Mass Loss with Aging Process. Age and Strength Loss." *Muscles, Ligaments, and Tendons Journal.* October–December 2013, 3(4): 346–350. https://www.ncbi.nlm.nih.gov/pmc/articles/PMC3940510/.

Kennedy, C., M.T. Bastiaens, C.D. Baidik, et al. "Effect of Smoking and Sun on the Aging Skin." *Journal of Investigative Dermatology.* April 2003, 120(4), 548–54. http://www.ncbi.nlm.nih.gov/pubmed/12648216.

Keys, A., A. Menotti, M. J. Karvonen, et al. "The Diet and 15-Year Death Rate in the Seven Countries Study." *American Journal of Epidemiology.* December 1986, 124 (6), 903–15. https://www.ncbi.nlm.nih.gov/pubmed/3776973.

Khalsa, S.B. "Treatment of Chronic Insomnia with Yoga: A Preliminary Study with Sleep-Wake Diaries." *Applied Psychophysiology and Biofeedback.* December 2004, 29(4), 269–78. http://www.ncbi.nlm.nih.gov/pubmed/15707256.

Kim, C.S., T. Kawada, B.S. Kim, et al. "Capsaicin Exhibits Anti-Inflammatory Property by Inhibiting IkB-a Degradation in LPS-Stimulated Peritoneal Macrophages." *Cellular Signalling.* March 2003, 15(3), 299–306. http://www.ncbi.nlm.nih.gov/pubmed/12531428.

Klein, G. Jean, PhD. "Using Healing Touch to Help Junior Nursing Students with Their Anxiety." *International Nursing Congress.* July 24–28, 2014. https://stti.confex.com/stti/congrs14/webprogram/Paper66977.html.

Kuttner, L., C.T. Chambers, J. Hardial, et al. "A Randomized Trial of Yoga for Adolescents with Irritable Bowel Syndrome." *Pain Research and Management*. Winter 2006, 11(4), 217–23. http://www.ncbi.nlm.nih.gov/pubmed /17149454?dopt=AbstractPlus.

"Lao Tzu's Four Spiritual Rules Of Living." Power of Positivity. https://www.powerofpositivity.com/lao-tzu-spiritual -rules-living/. Accessed February 12, 2019

Layne, J.E. and M.E. Nelson. "The Effects of Progressive Resistance Training on Bone Density: A Review." *Medicine and Science in Sports and Exercise*. January 1999, 31(1): 25–30. https://www.ncbi.nlm.nih.gov/pubmed/9927006.

Lebwohl, M., and L.G. Herrmann. "Impaired Skin Barrier Function in Dermatologic Disease and Repair with Moisturization." *Cutis*. December 2005, 76(6) (6 Suppl): 7–12. http://www.ncbi.nlm.nih.gov/pubmed/16869176.

LeGendre, O., P.A.S. Breslin, and D.A. Foster. "Oleocanthal Rapidly and Selectively Induces Cancer Cell Death Via Lysosomal Membrane Permeabilization (LMP)." *Molecular and Cellular Oncology*. January 23, 2015. http://www.tand fonline.com/doi/abs/10.1080/23723556.2015.1006077#. VOdArfnF-n9.

Leproult, R., G. Copinschi, O. Buxton, et al. "Sleep Loss Results in Elevation of Cortisol Levels the Next Evening." *Sleep*. October 1997, 20(10): 865–70. https://www.ncbi. nlm.nih.gov/pubmed/9415946.

Ley, S.H., Q. Sun, W.C. Willett, et al. "Associations Between Red Meat Intake and Biomarkers of Inflammation and Glucose Metabolism in Women." *American Journal of*

Clinical Nutrition. February 2014, 99(2): 352–60. http://www.ncbi.nlm.nih.gov/pubmed/24284436.

Li, Q., K. Morimoto, A. Nakadai, et al. "Forest Bathing Enhances Human Natural Killer Activity and Expression of Anti-Cancer Proteins." *International Journal of Immunopathology and Pharmacology.* April–June 2007, 20(2 Supplement 2), 3–8. http://www.ncbi.nlm.nih.gov/pubmed/17903349.

Lies, Shelby R., and Andrew Y. Zhang. "Prospective Randomized Study of the Effect of Music on the Efficiency of Surgical Closures." *Aesthetic Surgery Journal.* September 2015, 35(7), 858–863. http://asj.oxfordjournals.org/content/35/7/858.

"Lift Lighter Weights for Stronger Bones?" Berkeley Wellness. http://www.berkeleywellness.com/fitness/exercise/article/lift-lighter-weights-stronger-bones. Accessed March 11, 2019.

Lin, J.Y., M.A. Selim, C.R. Shea, et al. "UV Photoprotection by Combination Topical Antioxidants Vitamin C and Vitamin E." *Journal of the American Academy of Dermatology.* 2003, 48, 866–874. http://www.ncbi.nlm.nih.gov/pubmed/12789176.

Lindgren, L., S. Rundgren, O. Winso, et al. "Physiological Responses to Touch Massage in Healthy Volunteers." *Autonomic Neuroscience.* December 8, 2010, 158(1–2), 105–110. http://www.autonomicneuroscience.com/article/S1566-0702%2810%2900127-X/pdf.

Liu, Rui Hai. "Health Benefits of Fruit and Vegetables are From Additive and Synergistic Combinations of Phytochemicals." *The American Journal of Clinical Nutrition.* September 2003, 78(3), 517S–520S. http://ajcn.nutrition.org/content/78/3/517S.full.

Liu, Yang, and Marcia A. Petrini. "Effects of Music Therapy on Pain, Anxiety, and Vital Signs in Patients After Thoracic Surgery." *Complementary Therapies in Medicine.* October 2015, 23(5), 714–718. http://www.complementarytherapiesinmedicine.com/article/S0965-2299%2815%2900126-0/fulltext.

Lobo, V., A. Patil, A. Phatak, et al. "Free Radicals, Antioxidants, and Functional Foods: Impact on Human Health." *Pharmacognosy Review.* July–December 2010, 4(8), 118–126. http://www.ncbi.nlm.nih.gov/pmc/articles/PMC3249911/

Loftfield, Erikka, Neal D. Freedman, Barry I. Graubard, et al. "Coffee Drinking and Cutaneous Melanoma Risk in the NIH-AARP Diet and Health Study." *JNCI.* 2015, 107(2). http://jnci.oxfordjournals.org/content/107/2/dju421.

"Losing 30 Minutes of Sleep Per Day May Promote Weight Gain and Adversely Affect Blood Sugar Control." *Newswise.* March 5, 2015. http://www.newswise.com/articles/view/630723/?sc=mwhn.

Lucas, Michel, Fariba Mirzaei, An Pan, et al. "Coffee, Caffeine, and Risk of Depression Among Women." *JAMA Internal Medicine.* September 26, 2011, 171(17), 1571–1578. http://archinte.jamanetwork.com/article.aspx?articleid=1105943.

Ly, Jun, Lu Qi, Canqing Yu, et al. "Consumption of Spicy Foods and Total and Cause Specific Mortality: Population Based Cohort Study." *BMJ.* August 4, 2015, 351, h3942. http://www.bmj.com/content/351/bmj.h3942.

Ma, Chelsea, and Raja K. Sivamani. "Acupuncture as a Treatment Modality in Dermatology: A Systematic Review." *The Journal of Alternative and Complementary Medicine.* June 26, 2015. http://online.liebertpub.com/doi/abs/10.1089/acm.2014.0274?journalCode=acm.

Mandal, Ananya. "Obesity and Skin Problems." News Medical. http://www.news-medical.net/health/Obesity-and-skin-problems.aspx. Accessed February 12, 2019.

Mann, Steven, Christopher Beedie, and Alfonso Jimenez. "Differential Effects of Aerobic Exercise, Resistance Training and Combined Exercise Modalities on Cholesterol and the Lipid Profile: Review, Synthesis and Recommendations." *Sports Medicine.* 2014, 44(2): 211–221. https://www.ncbi.nlm.nih.gov/pmc/articles/PMC3906547/.

Maraki, Maria I., and Labros S. Sidossis. "Update on Lifestyle Determinants of Postprandial Triacylglycerolemia With Emphasis on the Mediterranean Lifestyle." *American Journal of Physiology—Endocrinology and Metabolism.* July 7, 2015. http://ajpendo.physiology.org/content/ajpendo/early/2015/07/07/ajpendo.00245.2015.full.pdf.

Mardinoglu, A., S. Shoaie, M. Bergentall, et al. "The Gut Microbiota Modulates Host Amino Acid and Glutathione Metabolism in Mice." *Molecular Systems Biology.* 2015, 11(10), 834. http://msb.embopress.org/content/11/10/834.

Markwald, Rachel R., Edward L. Melanson, Mark R. Smith, et al. "Impact of Insufficient Sleep on Total Daily Energy Expenditure, Food Intake, and Weight Gain." *Proceedings of the National Academy of Sciences.* April 2, 2013, 110(14), 5695–5700. http://www.pnas.org/content/110/14/5695. abstract.

Marta, I.E., S.S. Baldan, A.F. Berton, et al. "The Effectiveness of Therapeutic Touch on Pain, Depression and Sleep in Patients with Chronic Pain: Clinical Trial." *Revista da Escola de Enfermagem da U S P.* December 2010, 44(4): 1100–6. https://www.ncbi.nlm.nih.gov/pubmed/21337796.

Martin, Stephen A., Brandt D. Pence, and Jeffrey A. Woods. "Exercise and Respiratory Tract Viral Infections." *Exercise and Sport Sciences Reviews.* October 2009, 37(4): 157–164. https://journals.lww.com/acsm-essr/Fulltext/2009/10000/Exercise_and_Respiratory_Tract_Viral_Infections.3.aspx.

Martínez-González, M.A., C. Fuente-Arrillaga, J.M. Nunez-Cordoba, et al. "Adherence to a Mediterranean Diet is Associated with a Reduced Risk of Diabetes: Prospective Cohort Study." *British Journal of Medicine.* June 14, 2008, 336(7657), 1348–1351. http://www.ncbi.nlm.nih.gov/pmc/articles/PMC2427084/.

McConnell, Allen R., Christina M. Brown, Tonya M. Shoda, et al. "Friends with Benefits: On the Positive Consequences of Pet Ownership." *Journal of Personality and Social Psychology.* December 2011, 101(6), 1239–1252. http://psycnet.apa.org/psycinfo/2011-13783-001/.

McDevitt, Elizabeth A., Katherine A. Duggan, and Sara C. Mednick. "REM Sleep Rescues Learning from Interference."

Neurobiology of Learning and Memory. July 2015, 122: 51–62. https://www.ncbi.nlm.nih.gov/pmc/articles/PMC4704701/.

McNamee, David. "Metabolic Syndrome May Be Prevented by Healthy Gut Bacteria." Medical News Today. November 24, 2014. http://www.medicalnewstoday.com/articles/285962.php

"Mediterranean Diet Cuts Heart Disease Risk by Nearly Half." *American College of Cardiology.* March 4, 2015. http://www.eurekalert.org/pub_releases/2015-03/acoc-mdc030315.php.

"Mediterranean Diet Good for the Brain Too." MPR. October 23, 2015. http://www.empr.com/medical-news/mediterranean-diet-good-for-the-brain-too/article/448919.

"Mediterranean Diet Linked with Lower Risk of Heart Disease Among Young U.S. Workers." *Harvard School of Public Health News.* February 4, 2014. http://www.hsph.harvard.edu/news/press-releases/mediterranean-diet-linked-with-lower-heart-disease-risk/.

Meeker, John D., and Kelly K. Ferguson. "Urinary Phthalate Metabolites Are Associated with Decreased Serum Testosterone in Men, Women, and Children From NHANES 2011–2012." *Journal of Clinical Endocrinology and Metabolism.* August 14, 2014. http://press.endocrine.org/doi/abs/10.1210/jc.2014-2555.

"Microbes Help Produce Serotonin in Gut." ScienceDaily. April 9, 2015; http://www.sciencedaily.com/releases/2015/04/150409143045.html.

Miglio, Cristiana, Emma Chiavaro, Attilio Visconti, et al. "Effects of Different Cooking Methods on Nutritional and Physicochemical Characteristics of Selected Vegetables." *Journal of Agricultural and Food Chemistry.* 2008, 56(1): 139–147. http://pubs.acs.org/doi/abs/10.1021/jf072304b.

"More Coffee May Mean Less Endometrial Cancer Risk." MPR. February 6, 2015. http://www.empr.com/more-cof fee-may-mean-less-endometrial-cancer-risk/article/396947.

"More Reasons Why Getting a Good Night's Sleep Is Important." Newswise. March 26, 2015. http://www.newswise. com/articles/view/631841/?sc=mwhn.

Morris, Martha Clare, Christy C. Tangney, Yamin Wang, et al. "MIND Diet Associated with Reduced Incidence of Alzheimer's Disease." *Alzheimer's and Dementia.* February 11, 2015. http://www.alzheimersanddementia.com/article /S1552-5260(15)00017-5/abstract.

Moy, K.A., L. Jiao, N.D. Freedman, et al. "Soluble Receptor for Advanced Glycation End Products and Risk of Liver Cancer." *Hepatology.* June 2013, 57(6): 2338–45. http:// www.ncbi.nlm.nih.gov/pubmed/23325627.

Muizzuddin, N., M.S. Matsui, K.D. Marenus, et al. "Impact of Stress of Marital Dissolution on Skin Barrier Recovery: Tape Stripping and Measurement of Trans-Epidermal Water Loss (TEWL)." *Skin Research and Technology.* 2003, 9(1), 34–38. http://www.ncbi.nlm.nih.gov /pubmed/12535282.

Mukherjee, Sushovita, Mohammad Adnan Siddiqui, et al. "Epigallocatechin-3-Gallate Suppresses Proinflammatory

Cytokines and Chemokines Induced by Toll-like Receptor 9 Agonists in Prostate Cancer Cells." *Journal of Inflammation Research.* June 17, 2014. http://www.ncbi.nlm.nih.gov /pmc/articles/PMC4070858/.

Mullington, Janet M., Norah S. Simpson, Hans K. Meier-Ewert, et al. "Sleep Loss and Inflammation." *Best Practice and Research Clinical Endocrinology and Metabolism.* October 2010, 24(5), 775–784. http://www.bprcem.com/article /S1521-690X(10)00114-4/abstract.

Myers, Jonathan. "Exercise and Cardiovascular Health." *Circulation.* 2003, 107, e2–e5. http://circ.ahajournals.org/con tent/107/1/e2.full.

Najmi, Mahtab, Zahra Vahdat Shariapanahi, Mohammad Tolouei, et al. "Effect of Oral Olive Oil on Healing of 10–20% Total Body Surface Area Burn Wounds in Hospitalized Patients." *Burns.* October 8, 2014. https://www .sciencedirect.com/science/article/abs/pii /S0305417914002794.

"Napping Reverses Health Effects of Poor Sleep." Newswise. http://www.newswise.com/articles/view/629425/?sc =mwhn. Accessed March 11, 2019.

"New Evidence that Drinking Coffee may Reduce the Risk of Diabetes." *American Chemical Society News.* June 9, 2010. http://www.acs.org/content/acs/en/pressroom/press pacs/2010/acs-presspac-june-09-2010/new-evidence-that -drinking-coffee-may-reduce-the-risk-of-diabetes.html.

"New Study Confirms Listening to Music during Surgery Reduces Pain and Anxiety." *Queen Mary University of Lon-*

don News. August 12, 2015; https://www.eurekalert.or /pub_releases/2015-08/qmuo-nsc081115.php.

"New Study: Transcendental Meditation and Lifestyle Modification Increase Telomerase." Transcendental Meditation News and More. December 6, 2015. https://tmhome.com /benefits/study-tm-meditation-increase-telomerase/.

"Nothing Beats a Good Night's Sleep for Helping People Absorb New Information, New Research Reveals." ScienceDaily. http://www.sciencedaily.com/ releases/2015/04/150417085218.html. Accessed March 11, 2019.

O'Mathuna, D.P., and R.L. Ashford. "Therapeutic Touch for Healing Acute Wounds." *The Cochrane Database of Systematic Reviews.* 2003, 4: CD002766. https://www.ncbi.nlm. nih.gov/pubmed/14583953.

Oginska, H. and J. Pokorski. "Fatigue and Mood Correlates of Sleep Length in Three Age-Social Groups: School Children, Students, and Employees." *Chronobiology International.* 2006, 26(6), 1317–28. http://www.ncbi.nlm.nih.gov/ pubmed/17190716.

Okada, Haruko C., Brendan Alleyne, Kaveh Varghai, et al. "Facial Changes Caused by Smoking: A Comparison between Smoking and Nonsmoking Identical Twins." *Plastic and Reconstructive Surgery.* November 2013, 132(5), 1085–0192. http://journals.lww.com/plasreconsurg/ Abstract/2013/11000/Facial_Changes_Caused_by_Smok ing___A_Comparison.10.aspx

"One in Three Adults Don't Get Enough Sleep." Centers for Disease Control and Prevention. February 18, 2016. https://www.cdc.gov/media/releases/2016/p0215-enough-sleep.html.

"Optimistic People Have Healthier Hearts, Study Finds." Sharita Forest, Illinois News Bureau. January 8, 2015. https://news.illinois.edu/view/6367/204443.

"Oregon Study Confirms Health Benefits of Cobblestone Walking For Older Adults." ScienceDaily. June 30, 2005. http://www.sciencedaily.com/releases/2005/06/050630055256.htm.

Ovetakin-White, P., B. Koo, M. Matsui, et al. "Effects of Sleep Quality on Skin Aging and Function." *Case Western Reserve University.* https://media.cleveland.com/health_impact/other/Lauder%20Sleep%20Skin%20Study%202013%20IID%20Poster%20%202013%20final.pdf. Accessed February 12, 2019.

Owen, R.W., W. Mier, A. Giacosa, et al. "Phenolic Compounds and Squalene in Olive Oils: The Concentration and Antioxidant Potential of Total Phenols, Simple Phenols, Secoiridoids, Lignans and Squalene." *Food and Chemical Toxicology.* August 2000, 38(8), 647–659. http://www.ncbi.nlm.nih.gov/pubmed/10908812.

Paddock, Catharine, PhD. "Over-the-Counter Sleep Aids Linked to Dementia." Medical News Today. June 12, 2015. http://www.medicalnewstoday.com/articles/288546.php.

Pandrangi, S., and L.F. Laborde. "Retention of Folate, Carotenoids, and Other Quality Characteristics in Commercially

Packaged Fresh Spinach." *Journal of Food Science.* 2004, vol 69(9): 702–707. https://onlinelibrary.wiley.com/doi /abs/10.1111/j.1365-2621.2004.tb09919.x.

Papantonio, C. "Alternative Medicine and Wound Healing." *Ostonomy/Wound Management,* April 1998, 44(4), 44–50; http://www.ncbi.nlm.nih.gov/pubmed/9611606.

Parker, G., N.A. Gibson, and H. Brotchie. "Omega-3 Fatty Acids and Mood Disorders." *American Journal of Psychiatry,* June 2006, 163(6): 969–78; http://www.ncbi.nlm.nih.gov /pubmed/16741195.

"Partial Sleep Deprivation Linked to Biological Aging in Older Adults." *American Academy of Sleep Medicine.* June 10, 2015. http://www.aasmnet.org/articles.aspx?id=5622.

Patel, Sanjay R., Atul Malhotra, David. P. White, et al. "Association Between Reduced Sleep and Weight Gain in Women." *American Journal of Epidemiology.* November 15, 2006, 164(10), 947–954. http://aje.oxfordjournals.org /content/164/10/947.full.

Peeples, Lynne. "Study: Frequent Tanning-Bed Use Triples Melanoma Risk." CNN. May 27, 2010. http://www.cnn. com/2010/HEALTH/05/27/tanning.booth.melanoma/.

"Poor Sleep Associated With Increased Risk of Heart Attack and Stroke." *European Society of Cardiology.* June 15, 2015. https://www.escardio.org/The-ESC/Press-Office/Press -releases/Poor-sleep-associated-with-increased-risk-of-heart -attack-and-stroke.

Prado, Erick Tadeu, Vagner Raso, Renata Coelho Scharlach, et al. "Hatha Yoga on Body Balance." *International Journal of*

Yoga. July–December 2014, 7(2): 133–137. https://www. ncbi.nlm.nih.gov/pmc/articles/PMC4097898/.

Quan, Taihao, Tianyuan He, Sewon Kang, et al. "Solar Ultraviolet Irradiation Reduces Collagen in Photoaged Human Skin by Blocking Transforming Growth Factor-β Type II Receptor/Smad Signaling." *The American Journal of Pathology.* September 2004, 165(3): 741–751. https://www.ncbi. nlm.nih.gov/pmc/articles/PMC1618600/.

Quevedo, W. C. Jr., T. J. Holstein, J. Dyckman, et al. "Inhibition of UVR-Induced Tanning and Immunosuppression by Topical Applications of Vitamins C and E to the Skin of Hairless (hr/hr) Mice." *Pigment Cell Research.* 2000, 13, 89–98. http://www.ncbi.nlm.nih.gov/pubmed/10841030.

Quigley, Eamonn M. "Gut Bacteria in Health and Disease." *Gastroenterology and Hepatology.* September 2013, 9(9): 560–569. http://www.ncbi.nlm.nih.gov/pmc/articles/ PMC3983973/.

Raloff, Janet. "Dietary Protection for Sunburn (with Recipe)." ScienceNews. May 23, 2001. https://www.sciencenews.org/ blog/food-thought/dietary-protection-against-sunburn-rec ipe.

Ramanujan, Krishna. "A Cup of Coffee May Keep Retinal Damage Away." *Cornell Chronicle.* April 28, 2014. http:// www.news.cornell.edu/stories/2014/04/cup-coffee-day-may-keep-retinal-damage-away.

Rao, A. V. and L. G. Rao. "Carotenoids and human health." *Pharmacological Research.* March 2007 55(3), 207–16. http://www.ncbi.nlm.nih.gov/pubmed/17349800.

Rasch, Björn and Jan Born. "About Sleep's Role in Memory." *Physiological Reviews*, April 2013, 93(2): 681–766. http://www.ncbi.nlm.nih.gov/pmc/articles/PMC3768102/.

"Red Meat May Raise Young Women's Breast Cancer Risk." *Harvard School of Public Health News*. http://www.hsph.harvard.edu/news/hsph-in-the-news/red-meat-may-raise-breast-cancer-risk/. Accessed March 3, 2019.

Reynolds, Gretchen. "Phys Ed: Does Exercise Boost Immunity?" *The New York Times*. October 14, 2009. http://well.blogs.nytimes.com/2009/10/14/phys-ed-does-exercise-boost-immunity/? r=0.

Reynolds, Gretchen. "Younger Skin Through Exercise." *The New York Times*. April 16, 2014. http://well.blogs.nytimes.com/2014/04/16/younger-skin-through-exercise/?_r=0.

Rhodes, L. E., G. Darby, K. A. Massey, et al. "Oral Green Tea Catechin Metabolites are Incorporated into Human Skin and Protect Against UV Radiation-Induced Cutaneous Inflammation in Association with Reduced Production of Pro-Inflammatory Eicosanoid 12-Hydroxyeicosatetraenoic Acid." *British Journal of Nutrition*. September 2014, 110(5), 891–900. http://www.ncbi.nlm.nih.gov/pubmed/23351338.

Rivas, Anthony. "Drinking Coffee Can Lower Alzheimer's Risk By 20%, All It Takes is 3 Cups a Day." Medical Daily. November 26, 2014. http://www.medicaldaily.com/drinking-coffee-can-lower-alzheimers-risk-20-all-it-takes-3-cups-day-312410.

Rivas, Anthony. "How Does Smoking Cigarettes Make Your Skin Look Older? Twin Study Shows How Smoking Causes Premature Aging." Medical Daily. October 29, 2013. http://www.medicaldaily.com/how-does-smoking-ciga rettes-make-your-skin-look-older-twin-study-shows-how-smoking-causes-premature.

Rochester, Johanna R., and Ashley L. Bolden. "Bisphenol S and F: A Systematic Review and Comparison of the Hormonal Activity of Bisphenol A Substitutes." *Environmental Health Perspectives.* March 16, 2015. http://ehp.niehs.nih.gov/1408989/.

Rosendahl, A. H., C. M. Perks, L. Zeng, et al. "Caffeine and Caffeic Acid Inhibit Growth and Modify Estrogen Receptor (ER) and Insulin-Like Growth Factor I Receptor (IGF-IR) Levels in Human Breast Cancer." *Clinical Cancer Research.* April 15, 2015, 21, 1877. http://clincancerres.aacrjournals.org/content/21/8/1877.

Ross, A., and S. Thomas. "The Health Benefits of Yoga and Exercise: a Review of Comparison Studies." *Journal of Alternative and Complementary Medicine.* January 2010, 16(1), 3–12. http://www.ncbi.nlm.nih.gov/pubmed/20105062.

Rupani, Reena. "Probiotics for Healthy Skin." *Dermatology Times.* June 4, 2015. https://www.dermatologytimes.com/dermatology/probiotics-healthy-skin.

Ryan, Richard R., and Marylène Gagné. "Vitalizing Effects of Being Outdoors and in Nature." *Journal of Environmental Psychology.* June 2010, 30(2), 159–168. http://www.sci encedirect.com/science/article/pii/S0272494409000838.

Salem, Iman, Amy Ramser, Nancy Isham, et al. "The Gut Microbiome as a Major Regulator of the Gut-Skin Axis." *Frontiers in Microbiology.* July 2018, 9: 1459. https://www.ncbi.nlm.nih.gov/pmc/articles/PMC6048199/.

Sanchez, Albert, J. L. Reeser, H. S. Lau, et al. "Role of Sugars in Human Neutrophilic Phagocytosis." *The American Journal of Clinical Nutrition.* November 1973, 26(11), 1180–1184. http://ajcn.nutrition.org/content/26/11/1180.abstract.

Sanchez-Villegas, A., M. Delgado-Rodriguez, A. Alonso, et al. "Association of the Mediterranean Dietary Pattern with the Incidence of Depression: The Seguimiento Universidad de Navarra/University of Navarra Follow-up (SUN) Cohort." *Archives General Psychiatry.* 2009, 66 (10), 1090–1098. http://archpsyc.jamanetwork.com/article.aspx?articleid=210386.

Sanchez-Villegas, A., P. Henriquez, M. Bes-Rastrollo, et al. "Mediterranean Diet and Depression." *Journal of Public Health Nutrition.* 2006, 9(8A), 1104–9. https://www.ncbi.nlm.nih.gov/pubmed/17378948.

Sandoiu, Ana. "Just 20 Minutes of Exercise Enough to Reduce Inflammation, Study Finds." Medical News Today. January 16, 2017. https://www.medicalnewstoday.com/articles/315255.php.

Sarnoff, Deborah S., MD. "Can a Tanning Bed Safely Provide Me with the Vitamin D That I Need?" SkinCancer. 2011. https://www.skincancer.org/skin-cancer-information/ask-the-experts/can-a-tanning-bed-safely-provide-me-vitamin-d.

Scarmeas, N., J. Luchsinger, N. Schupf, et al. "Physical Activity, Diet and Risk of Alzheimer Disease." *Journal of the American Medical Association.* 2009, 302(6), 627–637. https://www.ncbi.nlm.nih.gov/pubmed/19671904.

Scheve, Tom. "Is There a Link Between Exercise and Happiness?" How Stuff Works. http://science.howstuffworks.com/life/exercise-happiness.html. Accessed February 12, 2019.

Schroeder, H., J. Marrugat, J. Vila, et al. "Adherence to the Traditional Mediterranean Diet Is Inversely Associated with Body Mass Index and Obesity in a Spanish Population." *The Journal of Nutrition.* 2004, 134: 3355–61.

Schulte, Erica M., Nicole M. Avena, and Ashley N. Gearhardt. "Which Foods May Be Addictive? The Roles of Processing, Fat Content, and Glycemic Load." *PLOS One.* February 18, 2015. http://journals.plos.org/plosone/article?id=10.1371/journal.pone.0117959.

"Severe Sleep Loss Affects Immune System Like Physical Stress Does." Medical News Today. July 2, 2012. http://www.medicalnewstoday.com/articles/247320.php.

Sforzo, G.A. "Opioids and Exercise: An Update." *Sports Medicine.* February 1989, 7(2): 109–24. https://www.ncbi.nlm.nih.gov/pubmed/2537995.

"Shin-Rin Yoku Means 'Forest Bathing'." Shinrin-Yoku. http://www.shinrin-yoku.org/. Accessed March 11, 2019.

"Significant Amount of Cancer-Causing Chemicals Stays in Lungs During E-Cigarette Use." ScienceDaily. Sep-

tember 10, 2018. https://www.sciencedaily.com/
releases/2018/09/180910142412.htm.

Silverberg, Jonathon I., and Philip Greenland. "Eczema and
Cardiovascular Risk Factors in 2 US Adult Population
Studies." *The Journal of Allergy and Clinical Immunology.*
January 8, 2015. http://www.jacionline.org/article/S0091-
6749(14)01677-7/abstract.

Sin, Nancy L., Jennifer E. Graham-Engeland, Anthony D.
Ong, et al. "Affective Reactivity to Daily Stressors Is Asso-
ciated with Elevated Inflammation." *Health Psychology.*
June 1, 2015. https://www.ncbi.nlm.nih.gov/pmc/articles/
PMC4666844/.

Sivamani, Raja K., Lori A. Crane, and Robert P. Dellavalle.
"The Benefits and Risks of Ultraviolet (UV) Tanning and
Its Alternatives: The Role of Prudent Sun Exposure." *Dermatology Clinics.* April 2009, 27(2): 149–vi. https://www.
ncbi.nlm.nih.gov/pmc/articles/PMC2692214/.

Sivertsen, Borge, Tea Lallukka, Keith J. Petrie, et al. "Sleep
and Pain Sensitivity in Adults." *PAIN.* August 2015,
156(8): 1433–1439. https://journals.lww.com/pain/
Citation/2015/08000/Sleep_and_pain_sensitivity_in_
adults.10.aspx.

"SkinCeuticals Unveils Novel Antioxidant Research." SkinInc.
August 11, 2015. http://www.skininc.com/skinscience/
ingredients/SkinCeuticals-Unveils-Novel-Antioxidant-Re
search-321418001.html.dpuf.

"Sleep and Sleep Disorders." Centers for Disease Control and Prevention. https://www.cdc.gov/sleep/index.html. Accessed March 11, 2019.

"Sleep Duration Linked to T2DM Risk." *MPR.* June 18, 2015. http://www.empr.com/medical-news/sleep-duration-type-2-diabetes-risk/article/421445.

"Sleep, Dreaming, and Well-Being." *Enlightened-Spirituality.* https://www.enlightened-spirituality.org/Sleep_Dreaming_and_Well-being.html. Accessed March 11, 2019.

"Sleep, Learning, and Memory." Healthy Sleep, Division of Sleep Medicine at Harvard Medical School. December 18, 2007. http://healthysleep.med.harvard.edu/healthy/matters/benefits-of-sleep/learning-memory.

Slominski, A., T.W. Fischer, M.A. Zmijewski, et al. "On the Role of Melatonin in Skin Physiology and Pathology." *Endocrine.* July 2005, 27(2), 137–148. http://www.ncbi.nlm.nih.gov/pmc/articles/PMC1317110/.

"Snooze You Win? It's True for Achieving Hoop Dreams, Says Study." Stanford Medicine News Center. June 30, 2011. http://med.stanford.edu/news/all-news/2011/07/snooze-you-win-its-true-for-achieving-hoop-dreams-says-study.html.

"SPF on Your Plate: Researcher Connects the Mediterranean Diet with Skin Cancer Prevention." ScienceDaily, American Friends of Tel Aviv University. August, 17, 2010. www.sciencedaily.com/releases/2010/08/100816122206.htm.

St. Helen, Gideon, Peyton Jacob III, Margaret Peng, et al. "Intake of Toxic and Carcinogenic Volatile Organic Compounds from Secondhand Smoke in Motor Vehicles." *Cancer Epidemiology, Biomarkers and Prevention*. November 14, 2014, 23, 2774. http://cebp.aacrjournals.org/content /23/12/2774.

"Strength Training Builds More Than Muscles." Harvard Health Publishing. https://www.health.harvard.edu/stay ing-healthy/strength-training-builds-more-than-muscles. Accessed March 11, 2019.

"Stress Can Shorten Your Life, an Oregon State University Study Shows." OregonLive. 2012. https://www.oregonlive. com/health/2011/10/stress_can_shorten_your_life_a.html.

"Stress in America: Generation Z." American Psychological Association. https://www.apa.org/news/press/releases/ stress/2018/stress-gen-z.pdf. Accessed February 12, 2019.

"Study Finds DASH Diet and Reduced Sodium Lowers Blood Pressure for All." ScienceDaily. December 20, 2001. https://www.sciencedaily.com/ releases/2001/12/011220082349.htm.

"Study: Physical Activity Impacts Overall Quality of Sleep." National Sleep Foundation. https://www.sleepfoundation. org/articles/study-physical-activity-impacts-overall-quality -sleep. Accessed March 11, 2019.

Swan, S.H., S. Sathyanarayana, E.S. Barrett, et al. "First Trimester Phthalate Exposure and Anogenital Distance in Newborns." *Human Reproduction*. February 18, 2015. http://humrep.oxfordjournals.org/content/ early/2015/02/03/humrep.deu363.abstract.

T., Satoh, Murata M., Iwabuchi N., et al. "Effect of Bifido-bacterium Breve B-3 on Skin Photoaging Induced by Chronic UV Irradiation in Mice." *Beneficial Microbes.* 2015, 6(4): 497–504. https://www.ncbi.nlm.nih.gov/pubmed/25809215

"Taking a Walk May Lead to More Creativity than Sitting, Study Finds." American Psychological Association. April 24, 2014; http://www.apa.org/news/press/releases/2014/04/creativity-walk.aspx.

Tanghetti, Emil A. MD. "The Role of Inflammation in the Pathology of Acne." *The Journal of Clinical and Aesthetic Dermatology.* September 2013, 6(9), 27–35. http://www.ncbi.nlm.nih.gov/pmc/articles/PMC3780801/.

Tarapore, Pheruza, Jun Ying, Bin Ouyang, et al. "Exposure to Bisphenol A Correlates with Early-Onset Prostate Cancer and Promotes Centrosome Amplification and Anchorage-Independent Growth In Vitro." *PLOS One.* March 3, 2014. http://www.plosone.org/article/info%3Adoi%2F10.1371%2Fjournal.pone.0090332.

Tchi, Rodika. "Feng Shui Use of Plants in the Bedroom." The Spruce. November 26, 2018. https://www.thespruce.com/plants-in-the-bedroom-1274803.

Tchi, Rodika. "Three Things That Make a Good Feng Shui Bed." The Spruce. February 14, 2019. https://www.thespruce.com/things-that-make-a-good-feng-shui-bed-1274335. Accessed March 11, 2019.

"Telemere Extension Turns Back Aging Clock in Cultured Human Cells, Study Finds." Stanford Medicine News

Center. January 22, 2015. http://med.stanford.edu/news/
all-news/2015/01/telomere-extension-turns-back-aging-
clock-in-cultured-cells.html.

Ten Brinke, Lisanne F., Niousha Bolandzadeh, Lindsay S.
Nagamatsu, et al. "Aerobic Exercise Increases Hippocampal
Volume in Older Women with Probable Mild Cognitive
Impairment: a 6-month Randomised Controlled Trial."
British Journal of Sports Medicine. April 7, 2014, 49(4).
https://bjsm.bmj.com/content/49/4/248.

Tilbrook, H.E., H. Cox, C.E. Hewitt, et al. "Yoga for Chronic
Back Pain: A Randomized Trial." *Annals of Internal Medicine.* November 1, 2011, 155(9), 569–78. http://www.
ncbi.nlm.nih.gov/pubmed/22041945.

Tipoe, G.L., T.M. Leung, M.W. Hung, et al. "Green Tea Polyphenols as an Anti-oxidant and Anti-inflammatory Agent
for Cardiovascular Protection." *Cardiovascular and Hema-
tological Disorders Drug Targets.* June 2007, 7(2): 135–44.
https://www.ncbi.nlm.nih.gov/pubmed/17584048.

"Understanding Chronic Stress." American Psychological Association. https://www.apa.org/helpcenter/understanding
-chronic-stress

"UVA and UVB." SkinCancer. May 24, 2013. https://www.
skincancer.org/prevention/uva-and-uvb.

Valderes-Martinez, Palmira, Gemma Chiva-Blanch, Rosa
Casas, et al. "Tomato Sauce Enriched with Olive Oil Exerts
Greater Effects on Cardiovascular Disease Risk Factors than
Raw Tomato and Tomato Sauce: A Randomized Trial."

Nutrients. March 2016, 8(3), 120. https://www.ncbi.nlm.
nih.gov/pmc/articles/PMC4808898/.

Vallath, Nandini. "Perspectives on Yoga Inputs in the Management of Chronic Pain." *Indian Journal of Palliat Care.* January–April 2010, 16(1): 1–7. https://www.ncbi.nlm.nih.
gov/pmc/articles/PMC2936076/.

Van Heijst, J.W., H.W. Niessen, K. Hoekman, et al. "Advanced
Glycation End Products in Human Cancer Tissues:
Detection of Nepsilon-(carboxymethyl)lysine and Arg-
pyrimidine." *Annals of the NY Academy of Sciences.* June
2005, 1043: 725–33. http://www.ncbi.nlm.nih.gov/
pubmed/16037299#

Vickers, Andrew J., Angel M. Cronin, Alexandra C. Maschino,
et al. "Acupuncture: In Depth." National Center for Complementary and Integrative Health. http://nccih.nih.gov/
health/acupuncture/introduction. Accessed March 11,
2019.

Wadyka, Sally. "Inflammation: Skin Enemy Number One."
YouBeauty. September 29, 2011. http://www.youbeauty.
com/skin/inflammation.

"Walking an Extra Two Minutes Each Hour May Offset Hazards of Sitting Too Long." University of Utah Healthcare.
April 30, 2015. https://healthcare.utah.edu/publicaffairs/
news/2015/04/04-30-15_short_walks_offset_hazards_of_
sitting_too_long.php.

Wang, Li-Shu, and Gary D. Stoner. "Anthocyanins and Their
Role in Cancer Prevention." *Cancer Letters.* October 8,

2008, 269(2), 281–90. http://www.cancerletters.info/arti cle/S0304-3835(08)00396-0/abstract.

Warber, S.L., S. Ingerman, V.L. Moura, et al. "Healing the Heart: A Randomized Pilot Study of a Spiritual Retreat for Depression in Acute Coronary Syndrome Patients." *Explore.* July–August 2011, 7(4), 222–33. http://www. explorejournal.com/article/S1550-8307(11)00099-1/ abstract.

"Watsu." Watsu. https://www.watsu.com/. Accessed March 11, 2019.

Wein, Harrison, PhD. "How Resveratrol May Fight Aging." *NIH Research Matters, National Institutes of Health.* http:// www.nih.gov/researchmatters/march2013/03252013resve ratrol.htm. Accessed March 18, 2019.

Westervelt, Amy. "Forgive to Live: New Research Shows Forgiveness is Good for the Heart." *Good.* August 25, 2012; http://magazine.good.is/articles/forgive-to-live-new-re search-shows-forgiveness-is-good-for-the-heart.

"What Happens When You Sleep?" National Sleep Foundation. http://sleepfoundation.org/how-sleep-works/what-happens-when-you-sleep. Accessed March 11, 2019.

"What is Bikram Yoga?" BikramYoga. https://www. bikramyoga.com/about/bikram-yoga/. Accessed March 11, 2019.

"What is Keeping Your Kids Up at Night?" Stony Brook University Newsroom. September 4, 2014. http://sb.cc.stony-brook.edu/news/medical/140904kidsupnight.php.

"What Should I Limit Sodium." The American Heart Association. http://www.heart.org/idc/groups/heart-public/@wcm/@hcm/documents/downloadable/ucm_300625.pdf. Accessed March 4, 2019.

Whitehead, Ross D., Daniel Re, Dengke Xiao, et al. "You Are What You Eat: Within-Subject Increases in Fruit and Vegetable Consumption Confer Beneficial Skin-Color Changes." *PLOS One.* March 7, 2012. http://journals.plos.org/plosone/article?id=10.1371/journal.pone.0032988.

"Who Wrote the Serenity Prayer?" *The Chronicle of Higher Education.* April 28, 2014. https://www.chronicle.com/article/Who-Wrote-the-Serenity-Prayer-/146159.

"Why Is Walking the Most Popular Form of Exercise?" *American Heart Association.* https://www.heart.org/en/healthy-living/fitness/walking/why-is-walking-the-most-popular-form-of-exercise. Accessed March 11, 2019.

Wientjes, Karen A. "Mind-Body Techniques in Wound Healing." *Wound Management and Prevention.* November 2002, 48(11), 62–67. https://www.o-wm.com/content/mind-body-techniques-wound-healing.

Willett, W.C. "The Mediterranean Diet: Science and Practice." *Public Health Nutrition.* 2006, 9 (1A), 105–10. http://www.ncbi.nlm.nih.gov/pubmed/16512956.

"Women's Study Finds Longevity Means Getting Just Enough Sleep." ScienceDaily. https://www.sciencedaily.com/releases/2010/09/100930161837.htm. Accessed March 11, 2019.

Wong, Cathy. "The Ideal Bedroom According to Feng Shui." VeryWellMind. February 21, 2019. https://www.very wellmind.com/feng-shui-tips-for-your-bedroom-88934.

Woolston, Chris. "Sleep Deprivation and Stress." HealthDay. March 11, 2015. http://consumer.healthday.com/ency clopedia/stress-management-37/stress-health-news-640/ sleep-deprivation-and-stress-646063.html.

"Worried About Prostate Cancer? Tomato-Broccoli Combo Shown to Be Effective." *ACES College News, College of Agricultural, Consumer, and Environmental Sciences.* January 16, 2007. http://news.aces.illinois.edu/news/wor ried-about-prostate-cancer-tomato-broccoli-combo -shown-be-effective.

"Yoga and Chronic Pain Have Opposite Effects on Brain Gray Matter." Newswise. May 15, 2015. http://www.newswise. com/articles/view/634072/?sc=mwhn.

"Yoga for Health." National Center for Complementary and Alternative Health. https://nccih.nih.gov/health/yoga/ introduction.htm. Accessed March 11, 2019.

"Yoga for Pain Relief." *Harvard Health Publishing.* April 2015. https://www.health.harvard.edu/alternative-and-comple mentary-medicine/yoga-for-pain-relief.

"Yoga, Running, Weight Lifting, and Gardening: Penn Study Maps the Types of Physical Activity Associated with Better Sleep Habits." Newswise. June 4, 2015. http://www.news wise.com/articles/view/635242/?sc=mwhn

Youngstedt, Shawn D., PhD. "Effects of Exercise on Sleep." *Clinics in Sports Medicine.* April 2005, 24(2), 355–65. https://www.sportsmed.theclinics.com/article/S0278 -5919(04)00139-5/abstract.

To Write to the Author

If you wish to contact the author or would like more information about this book, please write to the author in care of Llewellyn Worldwide Ltd. and we will forward your request. Both the author and publisher appreciate hearing from you and learning of your enjoyment of this book and how it has helped you. Llewellyn Worldwide Ltd. cannot guarantee that every letter written to the author can be answered, but all will be forwarded. Please write to:

Dr. Debbie Palmer
Valerie Latona
⅟ Llewellyn Worldwide
2143 Wooddale Drive
Woodbury, MN 55125-2989

Please enclose a self-addressed stamped envelope for reply,
or $1.00 to cover costs. If outside the U.S.A., enclose
an international postal reply coupon.

Many of Llewellyn's authors have websites with additional information and resources. For more information, please visit our website at http://www.llewellyn.com.